MW01621177

Christoph Wagner-Trenkwitz

A Sound Tradition

Christoph Wagner-Trenkwitz

A Sound Tradition

A SHORT HISTORY OF THE VIENNA PHILHARMONIC ORCHESTRA

Translation from the German
by John Hargraves

With 99 illustrations

To the memory of Ernst Ottensamer (1955-2017)

Visit us online at amalthea.at and wienerphilharmoniker.at

Original title: Das Orchester, das niemals schläft
Editing: Murray G. Hall
Cover Design: Elisabeth Pirker/OFFBEAT
Cover photo: The New Year's Concert 2017,
conducted by Gustavo Dudamel © Wiener Philharmoniker/Terry Linke
Graphic Design: VerlagsService Dietmar Schmitz GmbH, Heimstetten
Typeset in 11,5/15 pt Minion Pro
Designed in Austria, printed in the EU
ISBN 978-3-99050-109-2

Content

Foreword

This year, the year of 2017, our orchestra is celebrating a special birthday. One hundred seventy-five years ago the Vienna Philharmonic was founded in Vienna, that city of music which has always attracted and been home to important composers and musicians. This anniversary is an appropriate occasion to trace the traditions and present-day challenges of our orchestra in a literary way. The well-known Austrian writer on musical matters, Christoph Wagner-Trenkwitz, has taken on this task, and with the present book *A Sound Tradition* he has written a short history in facts, pictures and anecdotes. (The German title is *Das Orchester, das niemals schläft—The Orchestra that Never Sleeps*).

This same vitality that he ascribes to the orchestra in the original title is evident in his book. For Wagner-Trenkwitz takes his readers on a journey in a very charming and knowledgeable way. This way first leads us to a place where the orchestra was founded and which appears in the name of the orchestra as a sort of seal of quality: Vienna. If you take this walk through Vienna with the author you will meet music at every turning, and wherever you meet music, you will also discover traces of the Vienna Philharmonic.

But this journey with the orchestra leads the reader further: to the cities of Austria, first of all Salzburg, to the cities of Europe and indeed to cities all over the world. Here I would like to emphasize one city above all: New York, where a group of friends of the orchestra have united to form the Vienna Philharmonic Society. Its particular concern is also to celebrate the orchestra's 175th anniversary in an appropriate way. So the Vienna Philharmonic Society and the Vienna Philharmonic Orchestra created the idea for this book together, which is being published not only in German but also in English, so that many people from all over the world can participate in this literary-musical journey.

As the journey leads us to many different places, it also takes us to different times. Wagner-Trenkwitz takes us on a time journey from the orchestra's beginnings up to the present, and not just as a mere account of dates and facts, but in an informative, anecdotal, and occasionally humorous manner. We are witnesses to the great moments of Philharmonic history, but also to those times when the musicians and their music were caught under the wheels of ideology and racist fanaticism.

The author accompanies us into the world of a Philharmonic player, starting with his/her audition, going through the experience of being in the orchestra pit of the opera and on the concert stage, up through the schedules and challenges of a Philharmonic year. Wagner-Trenkwitz shows us the world of the great conductors and lets us have a look behind the scenes of the Philharmonics' everyday life with many a delectable story.

One of the special high points of the book is the chapter *Sound and Tradition*, in which the author takes a closer look at the mythic "Viennese Sound." The mystery of this acoustic experience is based on many components: the particular instruments, the special approach to tone, the particular kind of vibrato, the requisite orientation to the human voice in sound and phrasing that comes from daily playing at the opera and much more. The special ingredients of their success are the trust that the musicians have in one another and their familial spirit, which in the end are the guarantors of that special sound attested to by many and on which the orchestra's fame is based.

On the occasion of such a special birthday, it is incumbent on us to remember the beginnings. Whoever knows the principles of our founding fathers, who created the orchestra's standard of highest artistic quality, its democratic structure and sense of humanitarian responsibility, will understand why we feel bound to honor this tradition. But tradition remains alive only through innovation, and this is true both for its social responsibility and its artistic focus. Thus the book points out the thorough reappraisal of the orchestra's recent history, the artists' social responsibility regarding the pressing problems of our time, local and global initiatives for peace and international understanding, the equal treatment of men and women in the artists' collective, responsibility in creating programs with regard to contemporary music, the international recruitment of the next generation of musicians, and cultural education projects. Numerous activities of this kind show that the Vienna Philharmonic is, in the 21st century as well, an orchestra "that never sleeps."

Andreas Großbauer
Initiator of the book and Chair
of the Vienna Philharmonic Orchestra
in the Jubilee Year 2017

Greetings

The Vienna Philharmonic was founded in 1842. On the other side of the Atlantic, in the same year, without any coordination or consultation, the New York Philharmonic was also founded.

So both orchestras are celebrating their 175th birthdays this year (2017) and have had a close and friendly relationship for a long time—but not exactly since their founding. On March 28, 2017, there was a memorable birthday party for the Vienna Philharmonic at the Haus der Musik in Vienna (with representatives from New York in attendance) under the motto "Music knows no borders."

That is truly an apt motto. For music, which is not bound to language and which expresses every emotion, feeling, and thought common to mankind, indeed knows no borders.

In a speech I gave at this birthday party, I said that the music of Mozart or Beethoven, and of many, many other composers as well as their interpretations effortlessly crossed the borders into over 200 countries of this world. And more than a few of these "musical border crossings" have had their beginnings in Vienna, in Austria, and with the Vienna Philharmonic Orchestra.

Now a birthday party is a wonderful event; but it is just a "snapshot." For the date of a birthday slowly approaches, we look forward to it, one day it finally arrives, but in a very short time it is behind us again and is gone.

As opposed to that, a book is something lasting, something that one can pick up again and again, can give to someone else, and will have its fixed place on the bookshelf.

Admittedly, there have been excellent books, based on the latest research, that have been written about the Vienna Philharmonic in the last few years. I am especially referring to the standard works of Clemens Hellsberg (1992) and Christian Merlin (2017).

But the Vienna Philharmonic Orchestra is an almost inexhaustible topic, and so I was very pleased to hear that Christoph Wagner-Trenkwitz, as an outstanding expert on the music scene in general and the Vienna Philharmonic in particular, has taken his pen or keyboard in hand to write about "the Orchestra that never sleeps" on the occasion of the 175-year Jubilee of the Vienna Philharmonic.

Emperor Charles V. reigned, as we know, over an empire on which the sun never set. When we consider the fact that the Vienna Philharmonic gave 49 concerts abroad in the 2015/16 season alone and were on the move giving these concerts from Japan to the US and from Sweden to Australia, then we can truly say that the Philharmonic members are probably active all the times of the day (Central European time) and thus "never sleep."

And the best part is that the Vienna Philharmonic in the aforesaid period may have given 49 concerts abroad, but also 89 (!) concerts in Austria, and every single one of them at the highest standard.

I am proud of the Vienna Philharmonic and I wish this book, being published for the 175th Jubilee of this great orchestra, the greatest success.

Dr. Heinz Fischer
Bundespräsident (ret.) and
Patron of the Vienna Philharmonic

The Vienna Philharmonic Society

The Vienna Philharmonic Orchestra is known worldwide for its superb musicianship and unique sound. What is perhaps not as well known is that the Orchestra has a beautiful soul. Whether it is teaching children to play a violin, providing a safe haven for refugees to begin a new life or participating in the observance of a tragic event that must never recur—you will find the Vienna Philharmonic Orchestra leading the efforts to help, heal and herald new beginnings.

The Vienna Philharmonic Society was founded in 2016 to help the Vienna Philharmonic Orchestra bring its glorious music more often and to more cities across the United States. The Society is also bringing the values and ideals of this remarkable Orchestra to this country. A program of music education has already begun in New York for both public school children as well as advanced students in the music conservatories. That special Vienna Philharmonic Orchestra combination of musical magic and caring has been transplanted to the United States.

It is very moving to see such a talented group of musicians care so much about the problems of the men, women and children around them. Through its music and their strong philanthropy, the Vienna Philharmonic Orchestra makes a difference in many lives whether in Vienna, New York or Tokyo.

We invite you to join us as author Christoph Wagner-Trenkwitz brings to life the history and personalities of the Orchestra as it celebrates its 175th birthday. The English translation from the German original is provided by our board member John Hargraves.

Marifé Hernández
Chairman of the Vienna Philharmonic Society
New York, October 2017

THE VIENNA PHILHARMONIC SOCIETY

www.viennaphilharmonicsociety.org

Even if the orchestra does occasionally sleep, in the Musikverein the golden caryatids still keep watch.

A Tour

A Stroll through Vienna and through the History of an Orchestra

May I interest you in a little tour of the city? In less than twenty minutes, we will stroll by the most important centers of Philharmonic life of Vienna.

Home Base: the Musikverein

Let us begin with the Karlsplatz. Behind us, the baroque splendor of the Karlskirche, Ressel Park with its Brahms memorial, and the Technical University (formerly the Imperial and Royal Polytechnic Institute, where the Strauss brothers Johann and Josef studied). In front of us is the Musikverein building by Ringstrasse architect Theophil Hansen, who also designed the Vienna Parliament building, the Academy of Fine Arts at the Schillerplatz, the Stock Exchange on the Schottenring, and numerous palatial residences of the capital city. The home of the "Society of Friends of Music in Vienna" (*Gesellschaft der Musikfreunde in Wien*), founded in 1812, also houses the administrative offices of the Vienna Philharmonic Orchestra (or as it is called in good old Austrian bureaucratese, the "Chancellery.") Here, in the Great, or "Golden," Hall of the Musikverein, since it opened in 1870, the subscription concerts of the Philharmonic as well as the New Year's Day Concerts take place, which have contributed to its international standing.

Stars are set into the paving stones in front of the façade with the names of important musicians: the Austrian symphonic composer Anton Bruckner, the conductor Wilhelm Furtwängler, the contemporary German-Austrian composer Gottfried von Einem, and the Romantic Franz Schubert. These commemorative plaques are part of the "Vienna Music Mile." This memorial is quite neglected nowadays and certainly not a worthy "walk of fame" for the music metropolis, but can nonetheless serve as a reminder and orientation guide.

Going By the Ticket and Ball Office…

We cross Bösendorferstraße, bearing the name of the famed Viennese piano manufacturer, and walk down Dumbastraße (named for the Austrian industrialist Nikolaus von Dumba, who was vice president of the Musikverein and board member of the Vienna Men's Choral Association in the late 19th century), to the Kärntner Ring, where we will turn left.

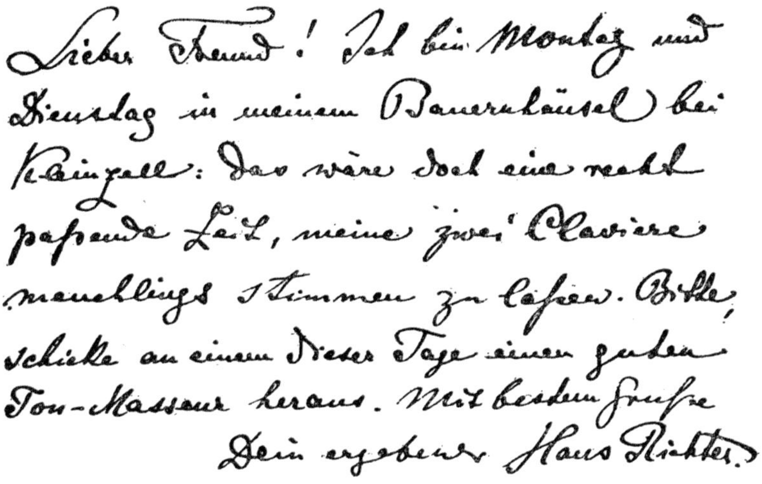
Lieber Freund! Ich bin Montag und Dienstag in meinem Bauernhäusel bei Kainzell: Das wäre doch eine recht passende Zeit, meine zwei Claviere manchlings stimmen zu lassen. Bitte, schicke an einem dieser Tage einen guten Ton-Masseur heraus. Mit besten Gruße
Dein ergebener Hans Richter.

Philharmonic conductor Hans Richter asks his "dear friend" Ludwig Bösendorfer to tune his pianos.

A few meters on from there we reach the Ticket and Ball Office of the Vienna Philharmonic, in front of which we see more music-stars: for Pierre Boulez, Johann Sebastian Bach and Johann Strauss. The Vienna Philharmonic Orchestra, the only musical organization so represented here, has a star commemorating its first concert on March 28, 1842. As we walk backward through history, we are now approaching this magical date.

Passing stars for Dmitri Shostakovich, Anton von Webern, and Herbert von Karajan (the plaque is graced by the maestro's signature as well, which Hildegard Knef thought looked like "a cardiogram"), we continue along the Ring to the State Opera building, rising to our right, and which, like the Musikverein, can be considered home base for our orchestra. For since its birth, the Philharmonic has recruited its players from members of the opera orchestra; aside from versatility, this provides economic viability for its musicians. A prerequisite for being accepted into the concert orchestra (organized as an association) is membership in the opera, which has a probationary period of several years. We will come back later to this "double identity" feature of our orchestra. For the moment, let us note that Philharmonic musicians, while playing in the opera, may not be called that, but should sound like it!

...and the other homebase: the State Opera

Only one year older than the Musikverein, the Court Opera Theater on the Ring was completed according to plans of the architects August Sicard von Sicardsburg and Eduard van der Nüll in 1869 and opened on May 25 with Mozart's *Don Giovanni* (back then presented in German as *Don Juan*).

The space to the right of the Vienna State Opera (as seen from the Ring) originally had no name, as it was part of Kärntner Straße. At the instigation of the then director of the State Opera, Ioan Holender, the tract was named Herbert-von Karajan-Platz in 1996. On the one hand, honoring the outstanding conductor and eminent house director (from 1956 to 1964) is quite appropriate; on the other hand, it makes one wonder how a half century after the end of the war, a square in the capital of Austria can be dedicated to a prominent former Nazi party member...A research group commissioned in the early 2010's by the University of Vienna and the city to deal with street names identified the Karajan-Platz as a "case needing further discussion."

Several more musical celebrities are remembered here with stars: the composers Alban Berg and Richard Strauss and their superb conductors Clemens Krauss and Karl Böhm. Then, lined up together, Giuseppe Verdi, Leonie Rysanek, Hans Knappertsbusch and, last but not least, Gustav

Mahler. Directly across from the side entrance of the opera house is the beginning of Mahlerstraße, a name it bore at first only between 1919 and 1938. It mutated under the Nazis to "Meistersingerstraße" until 1945 when the name and remembrance of the Court Opera director were restored.

The Kärntnertor-Theater—today Vienna's most famous Hotel

Behind the opera runs the Philharmonikerstraße, which was given that name in 1942 to mark the orchestra's Centennial Jubilee year. Crossing this street we find ourselves in front of the world-famous Hotel Sacher. It got its nickname—"Vienna's most musical hotel"—not just from the huge number of guests from "next door," but also due to its precise geographic location: from 1709 to 1870 the "Imperial and Royal Court Opera Theater by the Kärntnertor," the forerunner of the Opera on the Ring stood in this spot. If we just scan the decades before the founding of the Vienna Philharmonic, the Kärntnertor-Theater premiered performances of, among other things, a *Schauspielmusik* and a piano concerto of Wolfgang Amadeus Mozart, operas by Joseph Haydn, Antonio Salieri, Conradin Kreutzer, Carl Maria von Weber and Franz Schubert. Schubert's song *Der Erlkönig* was first heard here in 1821, and eight years later, Frédéric Chopin had his Viennese debut as a pianist in this theater.

The most significant moments in the house's history are associated with the name of Ludwig van Beethoven: the premiere of the final version of *Fidelio* occurred on May 23, 1814, and that of the Ninth Symphony on May 7, 1824. And both were performed by members of the orchestra that was to become the Vienna Philharmonic. The Viennese public felt such a close connection to this musically important site that when the Hotel Sacher was built on the same place, it was forbidden in writing to have any opera performance there.

We could turn right and go on along the continuation of Philharmonikerstraße (Walfischgasse no. 13 was once "Café Parsifal", frequented equally by opera cast, staff and audience members) but we shall instead stroll up Kärntner Straße. At the end of the block is Maysedergasse, named for the violin virtuoso Joseph Mayseder, who was both a "Concert and Solo performer" at the Court Opera Theater. He never became a member of the Philharmonic, but nonetheless appeared as a soloist in the orchestra's first concert. We turn right onto Annagasse, at the start of which we are greeted by a memorial star for Arturo Toscanini. The Italian "maestrissimo" shaped the history of our orchestra for only a few years: his debut in October 1933 marked the start of the guest conductor system at the Philharmonic. In early 1938, the fiercely democratic Italian decided to shun Austria, now joined to the German Reich by the *Anschluss*, and its top class orchestra.

The Haus der Musik

We saunter down Annagasse (passing by the Ristorante Sole, where artists and the public like to go after opera performances), at the end of which is the Haus der Musik. Here we come excitingly close to the founding moment of the Vienna Philharmonic: the composer and conductor Otto Nicolai lived in this building during his service as Viennese Hofopernkapellmeister (Court Opera conductor). A memorial tablet placed in 1942 (at the hundred year jubilee of his once-in-a-century idea to form a concert ensemble from the opera orchestra) shows Nicolai's portrait, the dates of his all-too-short life (1810-1849), and the date of the first concert he conducted (March 28, 1842—a date we shall not forget so quickly!) remind us of this music-historical milestone.

The text on the house on Seilerstätte opposite turns out to be much more flowery: the marble tablet commemorates the legendary dancer Fanny Elßler, who was born the same year as Nicolai, but lived until 1884, and whose fame became downright mythical. The inscription: "She was the smiling face of her century, one of those rare masterworks whom the creator weighs in his hands for many ages, before releasing them to life." The most frequently performed work of the 1823/24 season in the Kärntnertor-Theater was the magical ballet *The Fairy and the Knight/Die Fee und der Ritter*—and the record-breaking number of performances was due to none other than its star: Fanny Elßler.

Let us enter the Haus der Musik, the former "Palais Erzherzog Carl" in the Seilerstätte. It houses, among other things, the Historical Archive of the Orchestra as well as certain publicly accessible memorabilia from the rich history of the orchestra in the Museum of the Vienna Philharmonic.

On the first floor, we pass by displays devoted to the history of the Vienna State Opera before entering a room containing information on the history of the world-famous New Year's Day Concerts of the Vienna Philharmonic. To the right we are led into an imaginary concert hall, where visitors can experience the high points of the last New Year's Concert or the Summer Night Concert of the Philharmonic, on large-screen displays. To the left is the historic Hall of Mirrors. Here there is documentation on concert tours, honors and distinctions, the Vienna Philharmonic Ball and the orchestra's artistic collaborations with composers such as Johannes Brahms, Anton Bruckner, Gustav Mahler, Richard Strauss, Hans Pfitzner, Franz Schmidt and Alban Berg, using original objects.

One's eye falls on the batons of numerous prominent orchestra leaders—at first glance, that of Toscanini looks to be as long as the others. But if we recall that the Italian maestro used to use an especially long stick to conduct with, we look a bit closer—and in fact, the stick is broken off. This probably occurred as the result of one of its owner's legendary fits of rage...

The adjoining Nicolai Room has a special document of Austrian cultural history on display: the decree founding the Vienna Philharmonic (see page 27). It also contains the first photograph of the orchestra (1864) and pictures of Otto Nicolai, the violinists Georg and Joseph Hellmesberger and others. And last but not least, the program of the first Philharmonic concert...you surely remember the date!

1842—What a Year!

We could continue our wanderings onto Singerstraße; the inn "Zum Amor" once stood there, where, according to a romantic account, the founding of the orchestra is said to have occurred; then, around the corner in Grünangergasse, in the editorial room of the *Allgemeine Musik-Zeitung* the plan was in fact conceived to form the first professional "sound body" of Vienna to give independent concerts...But now it's time for a pause. If we put that mythic year of 1842 under a magnifying glass, it shows itself to be a most significant year. Let's pull out the most important dates:

On March 3rd, the "Scottish" Symphony of Felix Mendelssohn Bartholdy had its world premiere in Leipzig's Gewandhaus and was conducted by the composer. A short week later, on March 9th, Giuseppe Verdi's first international success, *Nabucco,* first appeared on stage at the Teatro alla Scala in Milan. Verdi was a fateful figure for Otto Nicolai in two senses: for one, the latter had rejected the (in his opinion) inferior *Nabucco* libretto ("endless raging, blood-letting, screaming, beating and murdering is no subject for me") and in so doing opened up a pathway for the younger Italian to world fame. And for another, Nicolai's greatest opera success, *The Merry Wives of Windsor*, was outmatched more than 40 years later by Verdi's masterpiece on the same subject, *Falstaff*, and—unjustly—eclipsed by it. It is no surprise to us that Nicolai could simply not abide the Italian's music: "He orchestrates like a fool [...he] must have a heart like a donkey's, and is truly in my eyes a pitiful, contemptible composer."

The scarcely thirty-year-old Verdi visited Vienna in April of 1843 and conducted his *Nabucco* at the Kärntnertor-Theater—and thus with the musicians of the Philharmonic Orchestra. They had already performed the world premiere of Gaetano Donizetti's *Linda di Chamounix* on May 19, 1842. It is noteworthy that the "Rossini-Craze" of the early 20's, that is, the rage for the composer of the *Barber of Seville*, was "reignited" two decades later with Donizetti. Back then, German opera played second fiddle in Vienna, even though its greatest master was already standing at the door: Richard Wagner's *Rienzi* was produced on October 20, 1842, at the Royal Court Theater of Dresden. It was not to have its first Austrian performance until May 30, 1871, in the "new" house on the Ring. Other new works of note in the year 1842: Michail Glinka's *Ruslan and Ludmilla* (December 9 in Saint Petersburg) and finally, on the last day of the year, Albert Lortzing's *Der Wildschütz* at the Stadttheater in Leipzig.

Arrigo Boito, the Italian composer and librettist (of Verdi's last operas, *Otello* and *Falstaff*, among others) was born on February 24 of 1842, the operetta composers Carl Millöcker, Arthur Sullivan and Carl Zeller on April 29th, May 13th and June 19th. Our orchestra had hardly any contact at all with the latter-mentioned composers; more, though, with the works of the Frenchman Jules Massenet, who was born on May 12th: his opera *Werther* had its world premiere in the Vienna Court Opera in 1892.

The birthday of a sister institution should be mentioned, which falls on the 2nd of April 1842: the "Philharmonic Symphony Society of New York" was founded on that day, thus making the New York Philharmonic just a few days younger than the one in Vienna and the oldest symphony orchestra of the USA. Two death dates will round out this musical review of 1842: Mozart's widow Constanze passed away on March 6 in Salzburg (a mere 51 years after her husband!) and the then celebrated composer Luigi Cherubini died on March 15th in Paris. When the Vienna Philharmonic, then still known as "Orchestral Personnel of the Imperial and Royal Court Opera Theater", gave its first concert, it included two pieces by the late composer in its program.

In the Nicolai Room of the Haus der Musik, we are in fact physically close to the founding of the Philharmonic, and we can hardly believe that at one time other "founding" dates were being talked about besides this year of 1842…but more of that in the next chapter.

Our ramble through Vienna from the Musikverein to the Haus der Musik

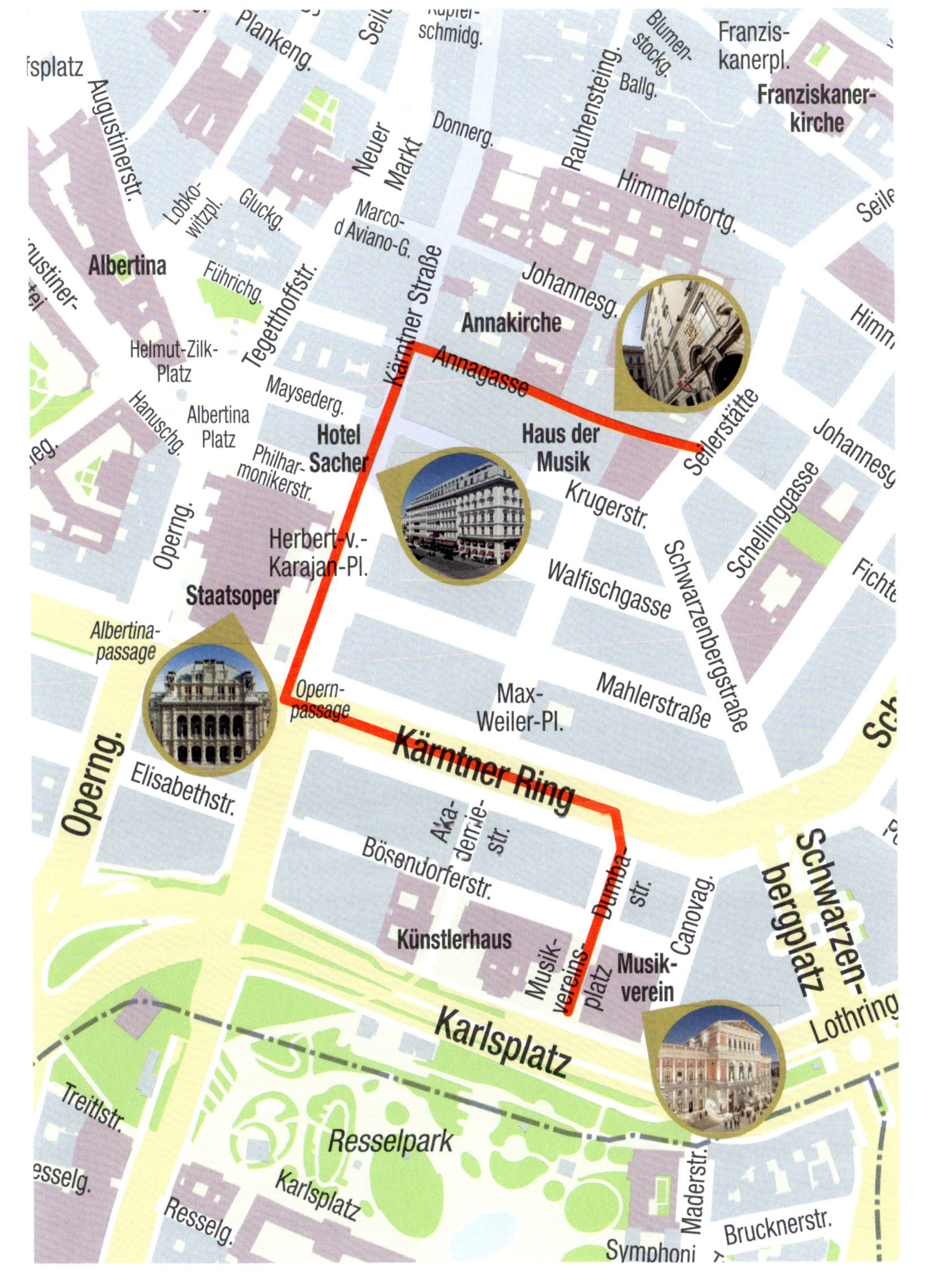
Plankeng.
Kupfer-
schmidg.
Blumen-
stockg.
Franzis-
kanerpl.
Ballg.
Franziskaner-
kirche
Augustinerstr.
Neuer
Markt
Donnerg.
Rauhensteing.
Himmelpfortg.
Lobko-
witzpl.
Gluckg.
Marco-
d'Aviano-G.
Albertina
Führichg.
Tegetthoffstr.
Kärntner Straße
Johannesg.
Annakirche
Helmut-Zilk-
Platz
Annagasse
Maysederg.
Hanuschg.
Albertina
Platz
Hotel
Sacher
Haus der
Musik
Seilerstätte
Johannesg.
Philhar-
monikerstr.
Krugerstr.
Schellinggasse
Operng.
Herbert-v.-
Karajan-Pl.
Walfischgasse
Schwarzenbergstraße
Staatsoper
Albertina-
passage
Opern-
passage
Max-
Weiler-Pl.
Mahlerstraße
Kärntner Ring
Operng.
Elisabethstr.
Aka-
demie-
str.
Bösendorferstr.
Dumba-
str.
Canovag.
Schwarzen-
bergplatz
Künstlerhaus
Musik-
vereins-
platz
Musik-
verein
Karlsplatz
Lothring
Treitlstr.
Resselpark
Resselg.
Karlsplatz
Resselg.
Maderstr.
Brucknerstr.
Symphoni

As a token of gratitude for the first Philharmonic concert, the orchestra presented Otto Nicolai with a portrait of himself (lithograph by Josef Kriehuber).

Old and New Home

Founding and Establishing the Orchestra (1842-1870)

After our tour of present-day Vienna, we will now journey into the history of our orchestra to discover more than one anticipation of the present. Today, it is almost impossible to imagine that in the first third of the 19th century, no professional orchestra existed in Vienna. Even Ludwig van Beethoven had to resort to amateur organizations for the performance of his symphonies.

The First "Ninth" and the "Künstler-Verein"

In many respects, the premiere of Beethoven's Ninth Symphony in May 1824 was the first signal flare of the Philharmonic idea. It took place in the Kärntnertor-Theater and was played by the house musicians, augmented by the Gesellschaft der Musikfreunde orchestra. We are reminded of the famous saying by Alexander Wunderer, the oboist and Board Chair of the Philharmonic: "We are the heirs of those who were taught by Beethoven." The event required two musical leaders, along with Beethoven himself, who by that time was completely deaf. It suffered from the fact that, as demanding a work as it was, it was allowed only two rehearsals with full orchestra and chorus.

The first attempt to found a professional concert orchestra in Vienna dates back to Franz Lachner. Like Otto Nicolai, who successfully founded a lasting institution nine years later, Lachner was a composer and leader of the opera orchestra. The "Künstler-Verein," or Society of Artists, which Lachner called into being from members of the opera orchestra, gave four subscription concerts in January 1833—however, due to faulty preparation, the undertaking was an economic failure.

"Kreuzdonnerwetter—Schwerenoth! Aufgewacht!"

Nicolai was the first to breathe life into the idea of a professional concert orchestra, with an energy and visionary pertinacity that could take on quite dictatorial traits. We have no record of the first orchestra meeting, but, miraculously, we do have the "Founders' Decree" from Nicolai's pen. It begins like a written, but very revved up, carnival manifesto: "Trin tin tin! Hark! Hark! The time has come, no more for musicians just to sleep, or play their violins in bed! Ye sons of Apollo, all together, unite, put your hands to work, on something great! Kreuzdonnerwetter—Schwerenoth! Aufgewacht!" (approximation: Hell and Damnation! Emergency! Wake Up!)

Then Nicolai gets to the point: "All Orchestra personnel of the Imperial and Royal Court Opera Theater and the Kärntnerthor-Theater, led by its good director Mr. Georg Hellmesberger, have united to give a concert under Kapellmeister N[icolai]'s direction, which will be unmatched in the annals of Viennese concerts." After a short program sketch comes this self-confident concluding paragraph: "Bravo Nicolai! And may the public encourage you in this endeavor, so that from this seed perhaps a beautiful tree will bloom!"

A Prussian from Königsberg, Nicolai had become Kapellmeister at the k. k. Hofoperntheater for a second time (after a brief intermezzo in 1837/38) in 1841. He celebrated his "comeback" in May of 1841 with a highly acclaimed production of his opera *Il Templario*. (This operatic rarity was recalled and earned enthusiastic reviews in the Salzburg Summer Festival in 2016.) His contract called for him to produce a new opera in Vienna, but it did not happen. The self-confident, all-giving, but all-demanding artist left the city in 1847 following a disagreement with management and the orchestra. Nicolai conducted the premiere of his *Merry Wives of Windsor* in Berlin on March 9, 1849, and died there two months later. For this native Prussian, Vienna could not be replaced by anything, as he confided to his diary: "Berlin probably has more order, which I missed so dearly in Vienna—but the Viennese has more music in his blood […] The south just has more talent!"

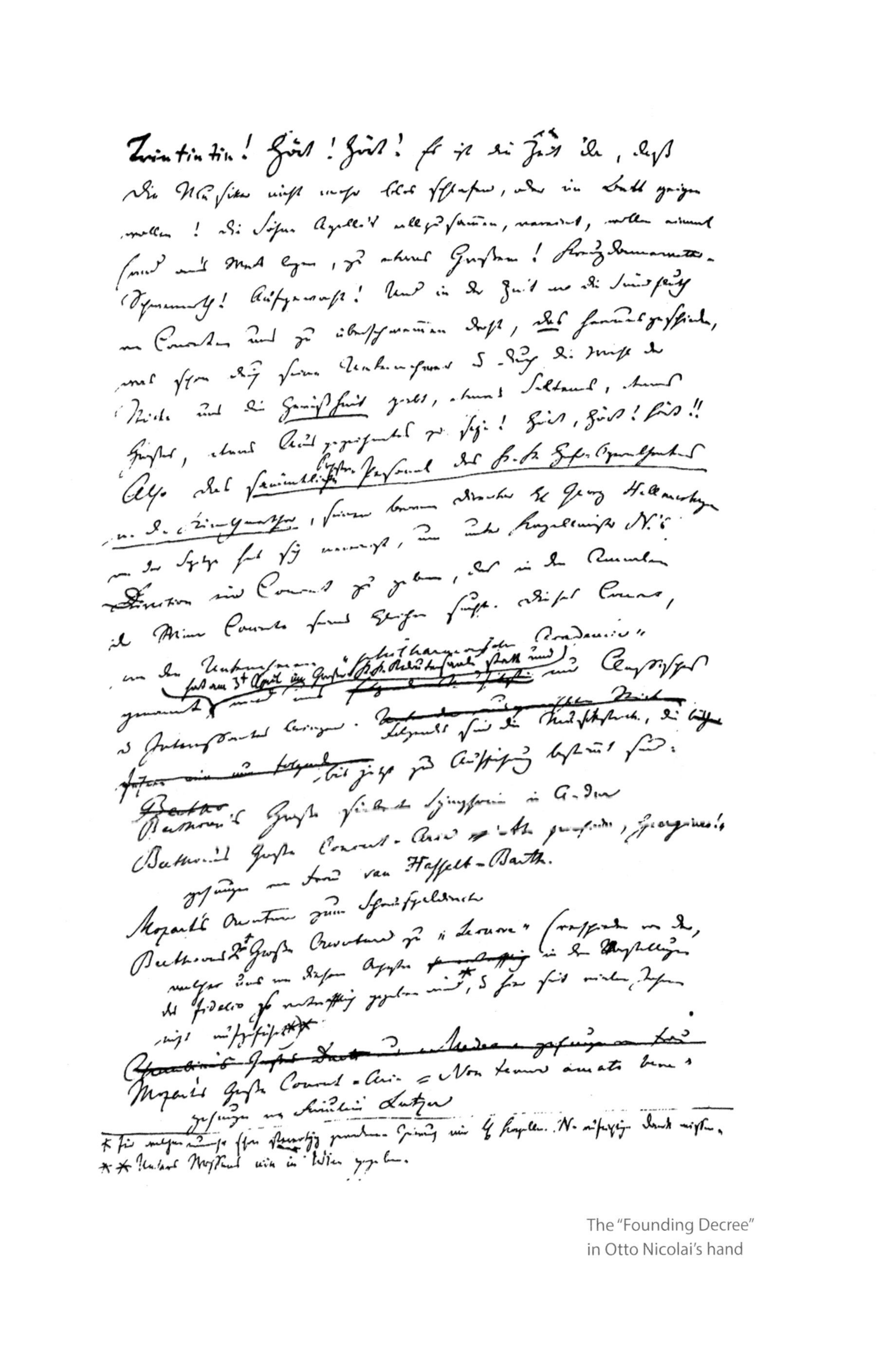

The “Founding Decree”
in Otto Nicolai’s hand

The Triad of Founders…

…of the Philharmonic, besides Nicolai, consisted of the Viennese writer and journalist August Schmidt (1808-1891) and the Manchester-born German Alfred Julius Becher (1803-1848). Schmidt was, among other things, a co-founder of the *Allgemeine Wiener Musik-Zeitung* (1841), of the *Wiener Männergesang-Verein* (Vienna Men's Choral Association, 1843), and the Vienna Singing Academy. It is to him we are indebted for writing down the motto which inspires the Philharmonic to this day, namely: "To give Philharmonic concerts in Vienna, whose purpose is to perform the best music with the best forces and in the best possible way." Dr. Becher's life and tragic end demonstrate that the founding of the Philharmonic also had a political dimension as a prerevolutionary democratic experiment: the composer and conductor became involved in the whirl of revolutionary events of 1848, became a public figure as the founder of the newspaper *Der Radikale* and was "executed by martial law" in Vienna on November 23.

Note that the Philharmonic idea was not imposed onto the opera orchestra from above but grew out of the collective body, which formed a committee to represent itself. Two dynamics were in play in the founding of the group: artistic necessity (to foster concert literature at the highest level, especially the Viennese Classicists Haydn, Mozart and Beethoven) and economic distress. Despite the great demand for it in the theater, it was in no way financially solid and barely secured in the social sense—there was not even a pension fund. According to Clemens Hellsberg, the income of an orchestra musician lagged behind that of a middle school teacher, an office trainee, or a well-paid factory worker.

The way and the means of founding the orchestra can be expressed in one word: autonomy. The freedom of personal responsibility and the concomitant flexibility in artistic and economic questions are ideals to which the Philharmonic has remained true to the present day. The same is true for the double-track duties in both the opera and concert enterprises, which often enough conflict with one another. An employee in the opera house, while an entrepreneur in the concert world: it is from this very tension that the members of the orchestra drew and continue to draw strength for great artistic achievement.

The First Concerts

The opera orchestra of 1842 did not even have half as many players as today's. While the State Opera in 2017 had 148 planned positions at its disposal, the number in Nicolai's time was exactly 64, and 31 of them were strings. Nicolai had to fill out his orchestra with "temps" from the Burgtheater and the Court Orchestra in order to succeed in the Great Redoutensaal of the Hofburg.

The first program, given on the "Easter Monday the 28th of March 1842, Midday at 12:30" (out of consideration for the opera, the orchestra could only have midday concerts on rehearsal-free Sundays and holidays) by "all the orchestra staff of the k. k. Court Opera Theater," started with Ludwig van Beethoven's Seventh Symphony. This *orchestra* "came into being to fulfill Beethoven's symphonic legacy," as Hans Weigel asserted. In addition, the master's first *Leonore* overture was played—not the third, as is noted on the program insert. Nicolai had already created a furore in the previous year with the third—the "great" *Leonore* overture: he had it performed between the two acts of *Fidelio*. "From now on, it will be impossible to perform *Fidelio* without it," he noted proudly in his diary.

With the presence of singers from the opera theater (they sang Mozart and Cherubini) and the cello virtuoso Adrien-François Servais, this first "Philharmonic" (which of course was not yet called that) resembled the orchestra "academies" that were common at the time, giving concerts with long mixed programs. In any event, the success of the concert was considerable, both artistically and financially. It brought in "an extra profit" that "the majority of the orchestra members needed," as Nicolai wrote to the opera director Carlo Balochino.

Nicolai continued on his path unflinchingly as the leader of the new concert undertaking and announced a "second Philharmonic Concert" for November 27, 1842 (the name was found, but would not be applied to the orchestra for a long time) in the Redoutensaal. Orchestral and vocal works by Mozart and Spohr were followed by Beethoven's Fifth Symphony. The co-founder of the Philharmonic, Dr. Alfred Becher, found prophetic words: "…It cannot fail to happen, with continued effort, that the Vienna orchestra will be the equal of the best in the world, and perhaps even superior to all the others."

Am Ostermontag den 28. März 1842,

Mittags um halb 1 Uhr,

wird das sämmtliche

Orchester-Personal

des k. k. Hof-Operntheaters

im k. k. großen Redouten-Saale

ein großes

Concert

folgenden Inhaltes zu geben die Ehre haben.

Erste Abtheilung.

1. **Die grosse siebente Symphonie** (in A-dur), von **L. v. Beethoven.**
2. **Arie** aus der Oper: Fanisca, von **Cherubini,** gesungen von Hrn. **J. Staudigl.**
3. **Concert-Arie** „Ah perfido, spergiuro!" von **Beethoven,** gesungen von Frau **van Hasselt-Barth.**

Zweite Abtheilung.

4. **Beethoven's grosse DRITTE Ouverture** zu Leonore, (verschieden von denen bei den Vorstellungen der Oper Fidelio im k. k. Hof-Operntheater aufgeführten.)
5. **Concert-Arie** „Non temer, amato bene," von **Mozart,** gesungen von Fräulein **Jenny Lutzer,** mit obligater Violin-Begleitung, vorgetragen von Hrn. **Joseph Mayseder.**
6. **La Romanesca,** Melodie aus dem 16. Jahrhundert, auf dem Violoncell vorgetragen von Hrn. **Fr. Servais.**
7. **Grosses Duett** aus der Oper: Medea, von **Cherubini,** gesungen von Herrn **F. Wild** und Frau **van Hasselt-Barth.**
8. **Grosse Fest-Ouverture** von **L. v. Beethoven.** (Op. 124. — C-dur.)

Die genannten Künstler haben die Ausführung ihrer Solo-Parthien, so wie Herr Kapellmeister **Nicolai** die Leitung des Ganzen aus besonderer Gefälligkeit übernommen.

Sperrsitze auf der Gallerie zu 3 fl.; Sperrsitze im Parterre zu 2 fl.; Eintrittskarten in die Gallerie zu 1 fl. 30 kr. und Eintrittskarten in das Parterre zu 1 fl. C. M. sind in allen Musik-Handlungen, an der Kasse des k. k. Hof-Operntheaters, und am Tage des Concertes am Eingange zu haben.

The first rules of order have not survived. Shown here are the rules of order from 1862.

ogram of the first
ilharmonic concert

On March 19, 1843, Nicolai took on the Ninth Beethoven Symphony, a repeat performance which became a moment of glory for him, thanks to the thirteen rehearsals which had been set for the demanding work: indeed, to some extent it became its "second world premiere" (Hellsberg). The Philharmonic ably demonstrated the "performability" of this symphony three years before its performance by Richard Wagner in Dresden.

Along with its relatively infrequent independent Philharmonic concerts and its daily opera duties, our orchestra continued to appear in numerous other presentations, mostly in the Kärntnertor-Theater. Thus Hector Berlioz directed the Philharmonic on December 16, 1845, for the first and last time, and his verdict was that "they might perhaps be equaled by other orchestras, but exceeded by none." When the composer Felicien David gave a guest performance of his internationally celebrated orchestral work *The Desert* in the Kärntnertor-Theater (it was only moderately successful in Vienna), our orchestra had to make do with a compliment that also contained a touch of critique: this "body" was "capable of doing anything"…"if only it wants to." We are reminded of a statement by Wilhelm Furtwängler, quoted by Board Chair Otto Strasser, which he made a century later after a concert in London, "that we were the best orchestra of the world—when we wanted to be."

In the 1840's, Franz Liszt and Robert Schumann were among the concert conductors while Friedrich von Flotow, Conradin Kreutzer and Giacomo Meyerbeer personally directed their own operas at the Kärntnertor-Theater—this close contact with the "great men" of their professions became the rule for the musicians of the Vienna orchestra from the first moment on.

Crisis and Farewell

For the eighth Philharmonic concert (March 30, 1845), Beethoven's Eighth was on the program—but someone other than Nicolai was at the podium. In February 1845, the conductor had become seriously ill, but the "ungrateful orchestra personnel," whose relationship with its strict chief conductor had not been without its frictions, refused to call off the concert. A musician from their own ranks was entrusted with the leadership: Georg Hellmesberger, a "guarantee of solid mediocrity" (Hellsberg). Once again it is noteworthy how history nearly repeats itself: When Gustav Mahler fell ill in 1901, the concert for March 1901 was given over to Joseph Hellmesberger, the grandson of Nicolai's orchestral director. Offended, Mahler resigned from conducting the concerts a little later. And for Nicolai, too, being "booted out" in 1845 was one of the reasons for his abandoning his "child." This came, of course, after some wrangling, and in full recognition that he had been the "leader of the best that Vienna can offer." Though the orchestra may have treated its founder unjustly, it honors his memory and name to this day with the annual Nicolai Concerts as well as the Nicolai Medal awarded for meritorious service to the Vienna Philharmonic.

On March 7, 1847, he conducted his eleventh and last Philharmonic concert with Mozart's "Great" Symphony in G minor, a Meyerbeer overture, and Beethoven's Second Symphony. Shortly thereafter, Nicolai bade farewell to the Kärntnertor-Theater with the "divine *Don Juan*, with which I accepted this position six years ago."

After Nicolai

In the opera there were also moments of glory, such as for instance the world premiere of Flotow's *Martha* on November 25, 1847, and the premiere of Meyerbeer's *The Prophet* under the composer's direction (after the closing of the Kärntnertor-Theater in the revolutionary years 1848/49), but the development of the Philharmonic Orchestra came more or less to a standstill in the "eleven lean years" (Hellsberg) following Nicolai's departure.

Nonetheless, the musicians of the orchestra continued to work as the "Gesellschaftsorchester der Musikfreunde" (Orchestra of the Society of the Friends of Music) under the direction of Joseph Hellmesberger, the distinguished violinist son of Georg, but had reached a "low point in their history" and were financially "almost exclusively dependent on the opera" (Hellsberg). This situation was partly due to the very arbitrary actions of the opera director Julius Cornet (appointed in 1853), who had little regard for the orchestra and overworked them, taking unfair advantage of the lack of a fixed rehearsal schedule.

One clash with Cornet deserves mention: first violinist Wilhelm Pauli was found on stage one day by the rabid director (who expressly forbade the musicians to set foot on stage during intermissions) and received this bawling out: "Get yourself back into the pit this instant!" Being addressed this way, Pauli answered him with the famous Götz quotation (from Goethe's *Götz von Berlichingen*, in English, literally: "K.M.A.! "), whereupon Cornet, in a fury, rushed up to the stage manager, Just, and screamed: "Did you hear what this insolent person said to me?"—"Yes."—"And what would you do?"—"Me, I wouldn't," said Just placidly.

In 1853, with the engagement of the opera conductor Carl Eckert, a phase of consolidation on the Philharmonic side of things also began. The violinist Henri Vieuxtemps and pianist Clara Schumann appeared as soloists, Liszt conducted the orchestra, and on March 25, 1855, the musicians first came into contact with a creation of Richard Wagner: the Prelude to Act III of *Lohengrin*. The Vienna premiere of the complete opera did not occur until August 1858 in the Kärntnertor-Theater.

The Philharmonic concert on March 1, 1857, under Eckert put a work by Schubert (Symphony in C major, D. 944) for the first time on the program of our orchestra. But what could have become a rebirth did not have any positive outcomes. Weaknesses of organization, publicity, and especially the "insufficient identification of the musicians with their project led to the temporary decline of the Philharmonic idea," (Hellsberg); only ten concerts had taken place in the decade after Nicolai's departure.

The "Rebirth"

It was nonetheless Eckert, who had been director of the opera since 1858, who would initiate the "rebirth" of the Philharmonic. On January 14, 1860, the Kärntnertor-Theater presented *The Merry Wives of Windsor* from the pen of the late founder of the Philharmonic (dead now some 11 years), and the next day the public was invited "at Noonday" to "the First Philharmonic Subscription Concert, presented by the Members of the Orchestra of the Imperial and Royal Court Opera Theater under the direction of Mr. Carl Eckert." The critic Eduard Hanslick was jubilant: "From the first note to the last, *one* spirit and *one* hand." Now that its time-tested quality was restored,

Concertmaster Joseph Hellmesberger, Senior, and conductors Carl Eckert and Otto Dessoff

the orchestra's new organization was a radical innovation which would well befit it going forward. Up to that point, the "Philharmonic" had indeed been marketed and sold as separate individual performances: the system of subscriptions (with only four concerts initially) gained the confidence of the public that crowded into the confined Kärntnertor-Theater to see "their" orchestra play on the stage set of that evening's presentation. Soon the subscription concerts were increased to eight, and to nine starting with 1864. This number was maintained for almost a century: not until 1961 was it increased to ten per year.

Eckert resigned his post for health reasons in 1860, and Matteo Salvi succeeded him as opera director. At a general business meeting, the Philharmonic members elected the twenty-five-year-old Saxon opera conductor Otto Dessoff to be its principal conductor, and there he stayed for a blissful decade and a half. "Dessoff laid the foundation for a house where later, perhaps more brilliant conductors came and went," write Herta and Kurt Blaukopf. "One cannot belong to the world of fashion without a subscription to the Philharmonic in one's pocket," enthused the newspaper *Der Wanderer* in 1864.

The 1860 introduction of subscription concerts was regarded until the 20th century as the founding moment of the Vienna Philharmonic. It was not until 1942 that it was decided to celebrate that year as the centennial of the orchestra's foundation by Otto Nicolai. But 1860 also marked the "creation" of a building that remains the home for our orchestra until the present day: the announcement of an architectural competition for the new Court Opera Theater that was opened nine years later.

Richard Wagner and the Vienna Philharmonic

The most important German opera composer, who first encountered the Philharmonic in 1861, deserves a more extensive digression, which will take us up into the 1870's.

Richard Wagner had revealed himself as a revolutionary and had to flee Dresden in 1849. As he had been declared a persona non grata in Germany, he now lived in exile in Switzerland. In May of 1861 he heard the orchestra of the Vienna Opera for the first time, and likewise his own *Lohengrin* as

Richard Wagner at a time when he was more interested in musical than political revolution

well. The maestro wrote to his wife Minna Planer, "for the first time in my difficult and painful life I have felt an unalloyed joy that is the conciliation for everything." This was succeeded a few days later by a no less acclaimed *Der fliegende Holländer*, after which Wagner announced in an address his plan to come to Vienna to rehearse his new opera: *Tristan und Isolde*. But after 77 rehearsals and the illness of the tenor Alois Anders the daring project of giving *Tristan* its world premiere in Vienna was abandoned. The composer, heavily in debt, had to flee his villa in Penzing. This "work of the century" first saw the light of the stage in Munich in July of 1865.

Worth mentioning is a world premiere that took place at the Kärntnertor-Theater, but without receiving the hoped-for acclaim. In February 1864, Jacques Offenbach's *Rhein-Nixies* was put on stage, from which years later the Frenchman took the most famous melody into his last work: the Barcarolle in *The Tales of Hoffmann*.

Wagner may have been disappointed by the opera administration's unwillingness to sacrifice everything for the world premiere of his *Tristan*; but he kept a lifelong feeling of affection for the Vienna orchestra, which was manifested as early as the 1862/63 season in several epochal, extraordinary

The first photograph of the Vienna Philharmonic (1864) on stage at the Kärntnertor-Theater. Center left is the conductor Otto Dessoff (in light trousers).

concerts. Excerpts from *Der Ring des Nibelungen* and *Die Meistersinger von Nürnberg* were heard in succession at the Theater an der Wien.

In May of 1872, just before laying the cornerstone at Bayreuth, the master guest conducted in the Musikverein, once again praising the Philharmonic in a rehearsal as "the best orchestra of the world," and adding, "Being with you and making music with you is a delight!" In a concert on the 12th of May, which also featured the finale of *Walküre*, a special effect occurred: just as Wotan summoned the fire god Loge to appear, a deafening thunderstorm broke out.

Some telling stories have come down to us about Wagner's visits to Vienna in March and May of 1875. The Court Opera singer Amalie Materna came to a rehearsal of excerpts from *Götterdämmerung*, exhausted from a prior rehearsal of Goldmark's *Queen of Sheba*. When she attempted to get through the rehearsal on half voice ("marking"), Wagner's reaction was: "Please don't mark! You can do your Goldmarking in the opera!" In the concert itself, it was yet again a Jewish rival who was detracting from his artistic energies. While the frenetically applauding public was trying to force the orchestra to encore the Funeral March from *Götterdämmerung*, the brass section members begged the maestro to spare them, since they had to play in Meyerbeer's *Die Afrikanerin* (*L'Africaine*) that night. Wagner explained the situation to the public and called the opera—whether erroneously or sarcastically is anyone's guess—"*Die Amerikanerin.*"

The one time Wagner conducted at the Court Opera was on March 2, 1876, at a benefit performance of his *Lohengrin*. The composer-librettist scattered roses in front of the concertmaster ("You play that so much better than I composed it"), but as an unpracticed Kapellmeister was able to depend on a "secret" sub-conductor, who thus prevented many blunders. This was no less a person than Hans Richter, the court Kapellmeister, who was devoted to Wagner: he took his place by the timpani and conducted at tricky places "with his drumstick, without Wagner being aware of it," as Joseph Sulzer, a contemporary witness in the cello section, reported.

After 1876, Wagner never visited the orchestra again, but it followed him: for many years, starting with the first Bayreuth festivals, members of the Vienna Philharmonic assisted in the festival orchestra. They were not all admirers of Wagner's "Music of the Future." Court Opera bassoonist Wilhelm Krankenhagen, e.g., noted in his *Götterdämmerung* part:

Der Zukunft Musik dereinst oben
Wird hoffentlich anders sein,
Sonst möcht' ich nach hiesigen Proben,
Nicht in den Himmel hinein.

(The Music of the future will be different in heaven,
I hope, than it is here at home:
If it's not, after all these rehearsals,
To Heaven I don't need to come.)

And Krankenhagen's *Parsifal* part contains these verses:

Zwei Knaben gingen nach Bayreuth,
Der eine dumm, der andre g'scheit.
Und als der *Parsifal* war um,
Da war der G'scheite auch schon dumm.

(Off to Bayreuth two boys went
One quite dull, and one intelligent,
But once *Parsifal* was done,
It also made the bright boy dumb.)

And second violinist Johann Czapauschek could not have been much of a fan either: Where Lohengrin confesses in Act I, "Elsa, I love you" he wrote into his part: "Here Czapauschek recommends an A major flourish from the brass, and *finis operis*!"

Living Composers and Historic Preservation

Back in the 1860s, important composers regularly stood at the podium of our orchestra, as for instance Max Bruch in concert or Charles Gounod, who conducted his opera *Roméo et Juliette* in the Kärntnertor-Theater. Celebrated concert soloists such as the pianist Anton Rubinstein and the violinist Joseph Joachim were also featured.

In 1865, the opera orchestra played to benefit the placement of a Schubert memorial (the monument by sculptor Karl Kundmann can be seen in the

Vienna Stadtpark today) and in the following year for a Mozart memorial, at which, as yet unpublished compositions of Rossini, that the composer had made available to the orchestra, were heard in the Great Redoutensaal. And finally in 1878, the orchestra volunteered to serve on a further memorial project: the Beethoven Monument by Caspar von Zumbusch was unveiled in 1880 on Lothringerstrasse, known today as Beethoven-Platz. The original model of the seated figure can be seen across the way in the Vienna Konzerthaus.

On the one hand, opera director Franz von Dingelstedt, appointed in October of 1867, campaigned for increasing the still meager orchestra salaries, but on the other attempted to bring the Philharmonic concerts under the Court Opera's control. "In the theater world, any independent organization working for its own private objectives is an anomaly that should not be tolerated, let alone protected," said Dingelstedt. But even if combining the opera with the concert business would have had resulted in "substantial alleviations in work conditions," the 'Philharmonic idea' and thus the Philharmonic itself would then have ceased to exist (Hellsberg). The orchestra stonewalled diplomatically, the new director decided to put off any sort of reform of this type until the time of the new house opening—and this moment was imminent.

The Opera House on the Ring

The new construction was not met with pleasurable anticipation. The plans were ridiculed, there was talk of things like "a sunken whale" and the "Königgrätz of architecture" (an allusion to the devastating defeat of the Austrian army at the Battle of Königgrätz in 1866). Even the architects' names were mocked in rhyme: "Sicardsburg und van der Nüll, they haven't any style" (in German, 'Nüll' almost rhymes with *Stil*, or style). Even artistically the new theater wouldn't work: In Blaukopf's account, "inside the house one could neither see nor hear anything."

In the end, these prophecies of doom were unjustified, and the Viennese public would soon learn to love the new house as much as they had the Kärntnertor-Theater. One egregious planning failure is noted by Hellsberg: "Foyers and coat checks for the orchestra were forgotten."

But there were also positive developments in the offing: in the autumn of 1868, anticipating the greater dimensions of the new house and the expanded demands of modern operatic literature, an expansion of the size of the orchestra was granted. For the first time, the organization exceeded 100 musicians, 55 new string instruments were purchased, and the string ensemble was significantly enlarged. For the first time, but by no means the last, the Philharmonic saw itself facing the problem of numerous new opera orchestra members also wanting to share in the concert orchestra "take," that is, the completely justified wish to participate in the "free" earnings.

As always, the Philharmonic concerts took place in the old Kärntnertor-Theater. The orchestra's petition to the General Management to allow it to use the newly opened (May 25, 1869) opera house for its "Philharmonic" concerts was denied because this building "as a matter of principle could not be used for any production furthering private interests." Dingelstedt engaged Johann Herbeck as a new Kapellmeister and forced the orchestra to compete with itself for the moment. Herbeck, the conductor of the concerts at the Gesellschaft der Musikfreunde since 1859, had long viewed the Philharmonic concerts revived in 1860 as competition; now, starting in November 1869 he was leading concerts in the opera house to benefit the Court Theater's pension fund.

One week later, Otto Dessoff conducted a "Philharmonic" concert in the Kärntnertor-Theater, which turned into a triumph: "The huge audience, occupying every space of the Kärntnertor-Theater auditorium, and the loud waves of applause after every number on the program, should have allayed any fears doubters might have had of the Philharmonic's concerts being endangered by any other new concert-giving organizations," announced the *Neue Freie Presse.*

When the Kärntnertor-Theater was cleared for demolition, the situation seemed to come to a head again: on April 17, 1870, the last performance (Rossini's *Wilhelm Tell*) in the old opera house took place, and the orchestra members had to remove their instruments within fourteen days. So now where were these tradition-filled concerts, loved so extravagantly by the Viennese public, to go now that the new opera house was closed to them?

The answer to this question leads us into a new chapter of Philharmonic history.

The "Golden Era"...

...began in the Golden Hall (1870-1897)

The beginning of the "Golden Age" for our orchestra is usually seen as 1875, when Hans Richter took over as the conductor of the subscription concerts. Although Hellsberg shares this viewpoint, he asks rhetorically, "Did this orchestra even exist before there was a Musikverein building?" in order to confirm his argument that the "international standing of the Philharmonic started in the 1870's." This ideal hall provided for "the full development of their (i.e., the Philharmonic musicians') sound potential" and put its enduring stamp on the playing of the Philharmonic musicians. The opulent interior configuration had a reverberation time of about two seconds and created the "warm" sound that favors lower frequencies. The financial stability of the enterprise is also worth mentioning: ticket income doubled in the short period from the last Kärntnertor-Theater concert in 1870 up to the 1874/75 season, which is additional justification for placing the start of the golden era at the orchestra's move into the Golden Hall in 1870. This has been home of the Philharmonic up to the present day and will hopefully stay that way in the future.

The conservatory had already moved to spaces in the new building on the Karlsplatz in the fall of 1869, and the concert halls opened in January 1870. Originally, the Gesellschaft der Musikfreunde had wanted to merge its orchestra into the Philharmonic, but this dissolution plan was likewise never realized. Our orchestra only made the concession of sending some of its musicians to play in the Gesellschaft's concerts. On Sunday, November 13, 1870, it was done: "the first Subscription Concert, performed by the members of the Imperial and Royal Court Opera Orchestra (still not "Vienna Philharmonic"!) took place in the "Great Hall," works of Weber, Beethoven and Schumann were on the program. Subscription series conductor Otto Dessoff, whose main job continued to be conducting at the opera, also started bringing international conductors in guest appearances for the "Philharmonic" players, including Hans von Bülow and Richard

Wagner. On December 29, 1872, Dessoff conducted his 100th subscription concert, and a few days before that, Emperor Franz Joseph had authorized the formation of a "Pension-Institute of the Imperial and Royal Court Opera Theater." The first Opera Ball took place on April 22, 1873—though not in the Ring building, but in the Vienna Musikverein. On this occasion, Johann Strauss the Younger conducted—violin in hand, of course—the world premiere of his waltz *Wiener Blut* (Viennese Blood). Just a few months later, at a Musikverein festival concert at the World Exposition in November 1873, Strauss conducted *The Blue Danube Waltz*. Those who enjoy the *Blue Danube* as an encore at the New Year's concerts should remember that the composer himself led one of the earliest performances of this "secret national anthem of Austria" with the Philharmonic players. This concert was made possible, incidentally, by the generous donation of the Chinese World Exposition Commission—it was to be another century before our orchestra toured China!

On October 26, 1873, Anton Bruckner conducted our orchestra in concert: the world premiere of his Second Symphony. Prince Johann II von und zu Liechtenstein had made available the means for a special concert: Arthur Nikisch, temporary first violinist of the Court Opera Orchestra, recalled "how Bruckner came to the podium, and then said to us (in his Austrian provincial accent), 'All right, gentlemen, we can rehearse as long as we want, I've got somebody who'll pay.'" Bruckner, highly elated by its success (the audience interrupted with thunderous applause after every movement, which was still "allowed" back then!), wrote a letter to the "Musikervereinigung" (musicians' association) asking "May I dedicate the work to you?" It is one of the dark spots in the history of our orchestra that they did not bother to reply to the composer, whose admiration for the orchestra they in no way reciprocated, for two years…

Paralleling the Philharmonic's high points—such as appearances of Franz Liszt and Johannes Brahms with the orchestra—were historic performances at the opera, too. On April 29, 1874, came the premiere of Giuseppe Verdi's *Aida*. At one rehearsal, there was tension between conductor Dessoff and his director Herbeck, who yelled: "the third flute is missing, Herr Kapellmeister, can't you hear that?" to which Dessoff replied: "the third flute is out today, Herr Direktor, can't you see that?"

Because he thought his opera salary insufficient, Dessoff left Vienna after fifteen years with a series of triumphal Philharmonic concerts, and even his adversary Herbeck resigned, "morally and physically half destroyed."

Within a few weeks, our orchestra gave concerts in the spring of 1875 under the direction of the two outstanding opera composers of the 19th century. After Wagner had given three acclaimed concerts, Giuseppe Verdi appeared in June to rehearse and conduct his *Requiem Mass* and *Aida*. To be sure, the latter did no "Philharmonic" concerts per se, but during a visit to the conservatory of the Musikverein he paid it a lasting double compliment: "With a school like this, Vienna will long have the first orchestra of the world." Hellsberg sums up the Wagner and Verdi visits and also the guest appearances of Brahms (of which more later) and Bruckner as follows: "The practical tests the orchestra passed as partners of great composers inspired that consciousness of tradition which lent a new dimension to the self-image of the Vienna Philharmonic."

A new Director, a new Chief Conductor

On May 1, 1875, a new Court Opera director took office: Franz Jauner did not hesitate to offer the opera to the Philharmonic for its concerts. Our orchestra never considered this offer again (with a few extraordinary exceptions at the end of the 20th century): "the physical separation of opera obligations and the concert business was final" (Blaukopf).

Along with Jauner also came a new 32-year-old conductor, to whom neither the opera nor the orchestra were new. Hans Richter was a native Austrian and former hornist in the Vienna orchestra. In 1866 he gave up his position in order to copy the *Meistersinger* score for Richard Wagner. This close connection lasted a lifetime: Richter was the best man at Richard's and Cosima's wedding, and he conducted the world premiere of the *Ring des Nibelungen* in Bayreuth in 1876 and its first performance at the Vienna Court Opera a little later. He died at Bayreuth in 1916 and is buried there. Richter was not only the leading Wagner conductor of his time, he was also leader of the Philharmonic concerts for a quarter of a century (with a short interruption).

As a former colleague, Richter did not enjoy the status of a detached, aloof magus at the podium, but rather that of a *primus inter pares*, as Arthur Nikisch later did, who had spent three years as a violinist in the orchestra, or like Willi Boskovsky, who while officiating as concertmaster led the New Year's Concert 25 times.

In his last letter to "his" orchestra (which he had left long before for a lucrative career in England), Hans Richter wrote in April 1913 that he must "gratefully acknowledge that I learned how to conduct from the orchestra. Of course, it has to be an orchestra as splendid as the Vienna Philharmonic; it is only in dealing with an orchestra like that you can learn what you can dare to do as a conductor."

Developing the Repertory

In the 1840's, Viennese Classicism played the dominant role in the programming of our orchestra, first of all Beethoven, who composed 60% of all the works performed. Johann Sebastian Bach was not in the repertory of those years, nor was Franz Schubert, who only "debuted" in 1857 with his "Great" Symphony in C major. Otto Nicolai had performed his own works only rarely. Rather, we find "stars" of the composer scene in the 19th century such as Cherubini, later Meyerbeer, Goldmark or Rubinstein—almost forgotten nowadays.

However, the "hostility" of the Philharmonic toward "modern" composers is a myth; in the 120 subscription concerts of the Dessoff era (1860-1875), 208 of the 265 works performed were new compositions. These were played through in so-called "Novitätenproben" (new work tryouts) and then voted on. Isolated new works would occasionally be accepted even "per acclamationem," that is, unanimous approval by applause, as for example the 1865 overture to *Sakuntala* by Karl Goldmark. The fact that certain other works of Brahms and Bruckner, for example, fell through the cracks may seem ridiculous from today's standpoint. In his first committee meeting as Chairman on June 4, 1875, Hans Richter cautioned that Hector Berlioz and Liszt were not getting enough attention; the former's *Symphonie fantastique* first found a slot in 1862, while Liszt had his last concert with the Philharmonic in January 1874 (the celebrated pianist played his *Hungarian*

Conductor Hans Richter dominated the "Golden Era."

Rhapsody and his orchestration of Schubert's *Wanderer Fantasy*). In the 19th century, the canonical repertory of today was still, while the works were brand new, the object of feuds and hostilities.

Let us take the now uncontroversial Peter I. Tchaikovsky as an example: the first work of his to be heard in the Philharmonic was the overture to *Romeo and Juliet* in 1876. Five years later, events led to a noteworthy Tchaikovsky world premiere, though rejected by public and critics alike: Adolf Brodzky, who had temporarily been a violinist in the Vienna Philharmonic but then decided on a solo career, gave the Violin Concerto its baptismal rites. Critic Eduard Hanslick, highly renowned to this day, having already rejected the works of Wagner and Bruckner, again demonstrated his limitations, aligning this work among those "pieces of music you can hear stink." The Russian was finally able to achieve posthumous recognition with the Vienna premiere of his 6th Symphony (*Pathétique*) in March of 1895.

Orchestra photo from 1865, the proudly bearded Hans Richter in the center

Difficult Rapprochement with Brahms

A work of Johannes Brahms, the Second Serenade, was heard for the first time on March 25, 1863, in a Philharmonic concert, of course with Brahms-fan Otto Dessoff at the podium. Despite the orchestra's several encounters with Brahms outside of the subscription series concerts, the reception of his works was sluggish: in 1869, the world premiere of his cantata *Rinaldo* reaped consistently bad reviews; at the end of the year, Brahms himself took over the conducting of a concert that Dessoff, threatening resignation, had refused. In January of 1871, the composer celebrated his comeback as a soloist in his First Piano Concerto and in 1873, he played his *Variations on a Theme of Haydn*. In 1877, the Philharmonic played a Brahms symphony for the first time and a world premiere at that: the Second Symphony, which according to the composer the orchestra "practiced and played with passion," was conducted by Hans Richter. The composer was present in the Musikvereinssaal, but his not standing to acknowledge the thunderous applause after every movement (!) was held against him.

Richter was able to push through the world premiere of the *Tragic Symphony* partly against the will of his orchestra and against that of the public, who left the hall in droves. In 1881/82 the Second Piano Concerto, the Violin Concerto and the Second Symphony were met with varying degrees of approval. Tensions about Brahms led to Richter's resignation as subscription concerts conductor. In the 1882/83 season Opera Director Wilhelm Jahn proved to be a help in time of need, managing to accomplish a partial world premiere of a Bruckner work (the Sixth Symphony).

The public and orchestra were not won over completely for Brahms until the world premiere of his Third Symphony on December 2, 1883, under the baton of the returned Hans Richter. He remained a loyal friend of the orchestra until the end of his life. At the 25-year anniversary of the Philharmonic subscription concerts, Brahms anonymously donated a sum of money "as a small token of cordial and grateful sympathy"—but the handwriting of the "anonymous" donor was recognized. In the end the Philharmonic gave the terminally ill composer a final gratification with a performance of his Fourth Symphony in March of 1897.

The composer
Johannes Brahms…

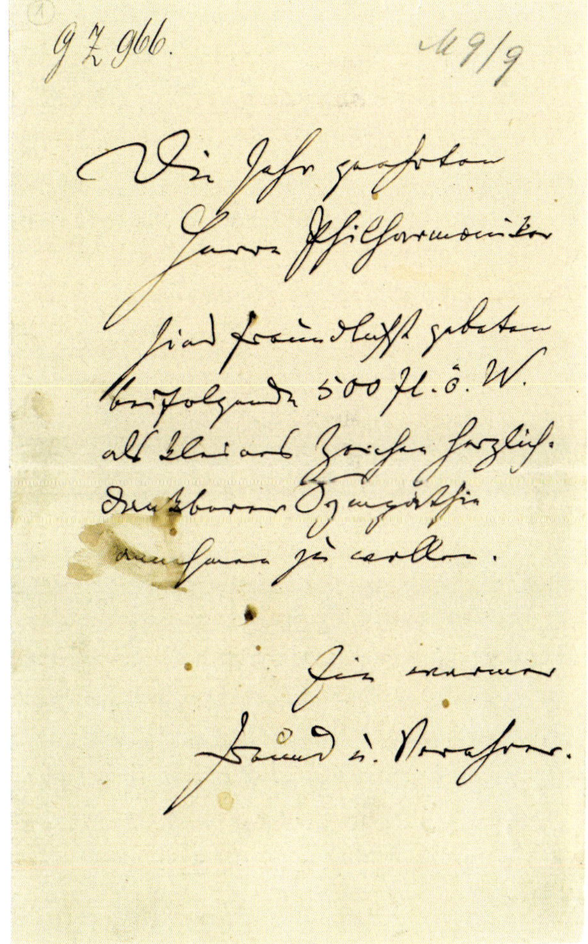

9 Z 966.

Die sehr geehrten
Herren Philharmoniker
sind freundlichst gebeten
beifolgende 500 fl. ö. W.
als kleines Zeichen herzlich
dankbarer Sympathie
annehmen zu wollen.

Ein warmer
Freund u. Verehrer.

…and his "anonymous"
500 gulden donation to
the orchestra

Where is Bruckner?

The Austrian symphonist Anton Bruckner was only accepted by our orchestra toward the end of his life. It world-premiered the revised First Symphony in December 1891, and a year later, it presented the second version of the Eighth, which Hanslick dismissed as "dream-confused hangover style." But the deeply touched Bruckner begged the members of "this highest artist association in music" to accept his thanks. Finally, in 1893, the Philharmonic collaborated with the Vienna Mens' Choral Society in yet another Bruckner world premiere, the chorus *Helgoland*. Bruckner also lived to see the inclusion of his *Romantic Symphony* in the subscription program of January 1896. He died on October 11th of that year.

He had not always had an easy time of it with his much admired Philharmonic. When Otto Dessoff suggested a list of new works in September 1874, compositions by Julius Zellner, Leo Grill, Robert Fuchs and Robert Volkmann were accepted, but Bruckner's Third Symphony was not. This work, dedicated to Richard Wagner, did not fare any better in 1875 or 1877; it was not to receive its world premiere until December 1877 under Bruckner's direction, but in a Gesellschaft concert of the Musikverein. At the end of the concert, the hall was "leergespielt" (played empty), which led Bruckner to the sad diagnosis, "the people don't care about my music."

In 1881, Hans Richter, outside of the subscription concerts but with the Court Opera Orchestra, had conducted the world premiere of Bruckner's Fourth Symphony, the "Romantic." Even in the rehearsals, the composer was filled with such childlike excitement that he pressed a guilder into Richter's hand with the words: "Drink a mug of beer to my health." This coin was to remain on Richter's watch chain for the rest of his life.

The opera director Wilhelm Jahn nonetheless conducted two movements from Bruckner's Sixth Symphony in their world premiere. In that same year, which was overshadowed by the passing of Richard Wagner, the first Vienna performance of *Tristan und Isolde* at last took place, over two decades after the unsuccessful attempt at a world premiere there.

In March 1886, Richter finally was able to do a complete performance of a Bruckner symphony in the subscription concerts. The Seventh was a considerable success, although the timid composer, fearing nasty critical reviews, had asked the orchestra not to do it. In 1890, the complete

The composer Anton Bruckner, first in an idealized portrait…

…then in silhouette: The composer is applauding his master interpreter, Hans Richter.

Bruckner thanking the orchestra in a letter of December 21, 1892, for the world premiere of his Eighth Symphony under Hans Richter.

Hochlöblicher Philharmonischer Verein!

Tief gerührt bittet der Gefertigte, es wolle ihm gestattet sein, sowol Sr Hochwohlgeboren Herrn Hofkapellmeister Dr Hans Richter, Ihrem bewunderungswürdigen, unübertrefflichen Leiter, als auch allen P.T. Mitgliedern dieses höchsten Kunstvereines in der Musik für die herrliche Aufführung seiner "achten" aus tiefstem Herzensgrunde zu danken! Hoch! Hoch! Hoch!

Wien, 21. Dezember 1892.

Dr Anton Bruckner

PHILHARMONISCHE CONCERTE.

Sonntag den 18. December 1892,

Mittags präcise 1/2 1 Uhr,

im grossen Saale der Gesellschaft der Musikfreunde:

4ten Abonnement-Concert

veranstaltet von den

Mitgliedern des k. k. Hof-Opernorchesters

unter der Leitung des Herrn

HANS RICHTER,

k. k. Hof-Opernkapellmeister.

PROGRAMM.

Anton Bruckner:

Symphonie in C-moll, Nr. 8.

(Sr. k. u. k. Apost. Majestät Kaiser Franz Josef I. gewidmet.)

(Erste Aufführung.)

Streich-Instrumente: Gabriel Lemböck's Nachfolger Carl Haudeck.

Programme unentgeltlich.

Text auf der Rückseite.

Das 5. Philharmonische Concert findet am 15. Jänner 1893 statt.

J. B. Wallishausser's k. u. k. Hof-Buchdruckerei.

The program from the world premiere

Sixth followed, but despite sporadic attempts until the composer's death to make up for past omissions, it is hard to disagree with Hellsberg's diagnosis of the orchestra's "crass neglect" of Bruckner until the turn of the century.

Hugo Wolf: Troublemaker

The young Hugo Wolf was a passionate Wagnerian and Brucknerian. He was equally emotional in his rejection of the works of Johannes Brahms, whom he termed the "greatest fake musician of the century." Starting in 1884 he gave vent to his likes and dislikes as a reviewer for the *Wiener Salonblatt;* he also condemned the operatic repertory, which was not on the same summit of quality as the orchestra: "Vienna possesses a precious vessel of an orchestra, but this vessel is filled up with bitter water, vinegar, lye, nitric acid, sulfuric acid and potassium cyanide."

It is understandable that *Penthesilea*, the symphonic poem Wolf submitted to the Philharmonic for their "new work tryout," did not receive a single vote. More than that, conductor Richter supposedly said over the musicians' howls of laughter after playing through the work, "I shouldn't have played it through to the end, but I wanted to have a look at the man who dares to write that way about *Meister* Brahms."

Hugo Wolf did not live to hear the world premiere of his *Penthesilea* in January 1910 under Felix Weingartner: in 1903, he died in a state of mental derangement.

"Light Music" and the "Discovery" of Salzburg

Richter invited the Schrammel family ensemble (two violins, guitar, plus clarinet or accordion, typically) to strike up some traditional Viennese music at the top of the orchestras's 100th Philharmonic concert—the "incomparable Viennese Waltzes of Josef Lanner [...]. Better than that I can't offer you..." Eduard Strauss expressed his indignation in a letter to his older brother Johann that Richter had not even mentioned the Strauss waltzes! Hans Schrammel was grateful for the friendly reception and expressed his thanks with two autograph works: he wrote a march for the Vienna Philharmonic, *Vienna Artists*, and another for the conductor: *The Hans Richter March.*

Johann Strauss had to wait until the Philharmonic presented a concert dedicated exclusively to his works. To celebrate the composer's fifty-year Jubilee, it presented a festive concert at the Musikverein on October 15, 1894, for which the composer announced his "fervent thanks to the great artists."

Two important dates in the orchestra's history, the effects of which are still unfolding today, took place in the "Golden Era." In spring of 1877, the Philharmonic made its first trip to its later "second home": the two concerts of the first "Salzburg Musikfest" under Otto Dessoff at the invitation of the "International Mozart Foundation" were not economically relevant, as they were played without remuneration—for food and lodging expenses. But this trip was the first guest performance of our orchestra, and the concerts could be considered the seed of the Salzburg Festival. At the Mozart centennial of 1891, the orchestra performed for the first time under the name we call it today: die Wiener Philharmoniker.

And, in the fall of 1886, the "Nicolai Association" was founded, a "Health Insurance Fund ('Kranken-Cassa') for the members of the k. k. Court Opera Orchestra." This fund of the Nicolai Association was absorbed two decades later into the Philharmonic's fund, but the Nicolai Concerts have been given annually from 1887 to the present day.

A Century Ends

The "second Richter era" lasted from 1883 to 1898 and exhibited "unmatched harmony between the leadership and the members, who decided not to exercise their democratic rights, since they wanted to entrust themselves to an outstanding personality" (Hellsberg). Richter confirmed this: "The Philharmonic has only one enemy, and it is not to be found in the newspapers or in the music stores, but in its own incorporation." But was abdicating democratic process the solution? We are reminded of Winston Churchill's statement that democracy is the "worst" form of government, except for all the others that get tried out from time to time…

Hans Richter determined the repertory, including the new music they presented, e.g. Jules Massenet, Michail Glinka, Camille Saint-Saëns and Antonín Dvořák. Brahms' Czech protégé made his place in history; among other things, he conducted the premiere of his own ballad for choir, soloist and orchestra: *Die Geisterbraut* (*The Specter's Bride*). He pushed open the door to the 20th century with performances of the tone poems of Richard Strauss from 1892 to 1898: *Don Juan, Death and Transfiguration,* and *Thus Spake Zarathustra.*

"Nothing changed in the organization or constitution of the orchestra from 1870 to 1900," Christian Merlin asserts in a lapidary fashion. But the "Golden Era," concluding with the century's end, was followed by a time of reform and upheaval. The passing of Bruckner (1896), Brahms (1897) and Johann Strauss (1899) marked the end of an era. In 1897 Wilhelm Jahn withdrew from the position of Director of the State Opera after 17 years (a tenure not exceeded until the 21st century with Ioan Holender).

His successor was a 37-year old conductor from Bohemia who had already made a name for himself in Prague, Leipzig, Budapest and Hamburg: Gustav Mahler.

A genius as director of the
Court Opera: Gustav Mahler

Mahler and the Consequences

The New Century (1897-1933)

The statement is all too familiar: "When the world ends, I will move to Vienna, everything happens ten years later there." But the 20th century began here—at least musically—three years earlier. With the Kaiser's decision of October 8, 1897, Gustav Mahler was appointed Director of the k. u. k. Court Opera and kept the position until December 31, 1907. At about the same time a master conductor was reforming the La Scala in Milan: Arturo Toscanini. Unconditional authority and regular fits of rage were common to both. Of course, Toscanini came without the all-consuming "second profession" of composer and enjoyed a life that was almost forty years longer than Mahler's.

Vienna 1900

The composer Egon Wellesz described the cultural atmosphere of Vienna at the turn of the century as follows: "There is something mysterious in the flourishing of intellectual and spiritual life of a people in times, unimagined by most, that their country is drifting toward catastrophe. Turn of the century Austria gave, and Vienna took, writers, poets, painters, sculptors, architects and musicians in an abundance which made this epoch one of the greatest in the history of the country and of this city. This was the atmosphere in which a musician with the greatness of Gustav Mahler could make the Vienna Opera the first opera stage of Europe, could make the orchestra his infallible instrument, and could make the public his public, to be transported by him from experience to experience."

"Vienna 1900" remained the embodiment of a culturally pulsating, multi-ethnic metropolis—half the people living in the capital, including Mahler, were not born here—, the musical aspect of which Mahler exemplified: as a charismatic director and composer, idolized by the young but crassly undervalued by many. When the Philharmonic played Mahler's First Symphony in 1900, Hanslick, notorious for his critical misjudgments, said caustically: "One of us must be crazy—and it's not me!"

A few jokesters have immortalized themselves in the Philharmonic part scores for Mahler's Second Symphony. To the performance direction for the start of the first movement, "With absolute seriousness and solemnity of expression", one violinist added "on your face". And the "Great Appeal" (*Große Appell*) in the fifth movement inspired a bassoonist to change it to *Großer Rappel* (Great Tantrum), a violinist to *Saurer Apfel* (Sour Apple) and a cellist to *Großer Roß-Apfel* (Great Horse-Apple).

Is Tradition Sloppiness?

Here we are less interested in the misjudged composer-genius than in the person of Mahler as director of the Court Opera, who touched off so many earthquakes in the capital's temple of art. Certain abbreviated catchphrases such as "Tradition is Sloppiness" reflect his position falsely. His phrase was actually "What you call tradition is often just sloppiness." The experienced musician knew exactly what was meant by real tradition, but he had no sympathy for faulty performance, and he demanded the utmost of himself and all his subordinates: thus there were almost seventy Wagner performances in the 1900/01 season at the Vienna Opera!

Many of Mahler's innovations were uncontroversial and practical. For example, his predecessor Jahn used to sit on a round cane chair in the middle of the orchestra, close to the performers on stage but having almost no contact with the strings. Mahler raised the conductor's desk and shifted it to the current position at the edge of the orchestra pit.

His idea (which was never carried out) to require the orchestra players to wear tails every night did no more for the "new" man's popularity than the wave of forced retirements he initiated. In his second season (1898/99) alone, 20 players were moved to the pension rolls. These were necessary because of the aging of the orchestra, as Merlin documents with this personnel highlight: the "solo cellos had not been changed for 25 years and the viola, double bass and flute soloists not for 28."

Mahler brought about a turnover in personnel never seen before. During his ten year tenure, he hired around 79 new orchestra members, "including of course some brief intermezzi" (Merlin). Thus, ten of the 33 brass players he brought on left before the end of his era. A great many of those who stayed left their special imprint on the orchestra, like the later concertmaster Franz Mairecker, the solo cellist Friedrich Buxbaum, the oboist Alexander Wunderer and the solo hornist Karl Stiegler. Mahler also opened up the orchestra by engaging numerous international musicians, from Germany and Holland in particular. Many a new member found his way into the orchestra without an audition, such as the trombonist Franz Dreyer, who had proved his worth at the 1902 world premiere of Mahler's Third Symphony in Krefeld.

Partly due to the retirements, partly because of conflicts with the all-powerful director, Mahler lost one harpist after another, so he cast an eye on Alfred Holy, who was a member of the Royal Prussian Opera Theater in Berlin. He sent his assistant Bruno Walter to Bayreuth as a negotiator, where Holy was assisting in the festival orchestra. As the story goes, their secret interview took place behind some shrubbery—successfully: Holy transferred to Vienna. Bruno Walter, who was one of Mahler's new hires himself, was to become a particular favorite of the orchestra over the decades. The Berlin native was actually named Bruno Schlesinger, which is why the conductor and later State Opera director Franz Schalk used to call him "Schlesinger von der Vogelweide..." [perhaps the most well-known medieval lyric poet in German was Walter von der Vogelweide. (tr.)].

Showdowns

In the 1901/02 season, in the course of a much needed expansion of the orchestra, things came to a showdown. Mahler had promised several newly engaged members of the opera orchestra that they would automatically be members of the Philharmonic as well; but at the next general meeting of the orchestra, this was voted down. Opera director Mahler fought back, and not only with words ("For me there is only a Court Opera Orchestra, I don't know any Philharmonic Orchestra"), but also with a concrete threat, to require the Philharmonic members to get permission from the General

Max Oppenheimer painted *Das Orchester* between 1935 and 1952 in exile in New York. Gustav Mahler, standing at the podium, as well as other figures shown here, such as Arnold Rosé and solo cellist Friedrich Buxbaum, had died long before the picture was finished.

Management of the Court Theater for their Philharmonic activities. But management sided with the orchestra and funded the hiring of new members in the Philharmonic. The Philharmonic statutes were altered for this: the maximum number of players remained at 108, but the so-called "Expektanten" would be admitted into the orchestra as soon as a place was free.

Mahler was a stickler for discipline. The oboist Johann Strasky, for instance, was forced to pay a fine for standing up in the middle of a ballet performance to check out a dancer's legs. Strasky really was a Viennese "original." He owned a tame goat, which he led around on a leash, and had had a position as a conductor in the suburb of Meidling (today in the 12th district) in the Richter era. In the district's "Katharinenhalle", along with vaudeville performances, circus shows and wrestling matches, you could also hear Haydn's *Creation* and Beethoven's Ninth Symphony under Strasky's baton! Hans Richter heard about the musician's success and congratulated him. Strasky thanked him, pointing out that he had not known at all how simple it was to "beat time." "A single wrong note from the oboe and the whole opera house hears it. But if you mis-conduct, not a soul hears it! The stick doesn't make a sound!" Richter replied with aplomb: "I've known that all along...but don't tell anyone else!"

As a musician, concertmaster Arnold Rosé was highly esteemed by the director, and by marrying his sister Justine in 1902, Rosé became Mahler's brother-in-law to boot. As "orchestra inspector" Rosé was responsible for discipline in the pit. On one occasion, his disapproving gaze fell on the bassist Franz Simandl, but the latter was unperturbed, loudly telling his colleagues, "It's no matter. What does Rosé know about the bass...". One time a performance of Mahler's First Symphony in Brno, conducted by the composer, was the cause of a blatant violation of discipline: six musicians, led by Arnold Rosé, took part in the performance, but bassist Otto Stix had probably neglected to ask for leave: he left the stage during a Philharmonic concert to go to Brno, which resulted in a disciplinary hearing against him.

Mahler's impatience with the musicians was legendary ("If some-one doesn't play just what's written, I could murder him on the spot") and known to the newspapers as well. One learned from the *Pester Lloyd* newspaper on November 16, 1898, that "many members of the

Arnold Rosé, Mahler's brother-in-law and his closest intimate in the Court Opera

orchestra are feeling harried by the excessive number of rehearsals that have been recently imposed on them, and perhaps also by the somewhat rude manner of their temperamental Director toward a few refractory members."

The oboist Alexander Wunderer described the Mahler phenomenon as follows: "The amazing thing was that we were making music as it was written in the score, and that this seemed to us to be something completely new. You have to know the theater business to know how big a role is played by routine, sloppiness and carelessness…and moreover, up to that point, the work of the conductor and the stage director were two separate domains; Mahler combined them all in himself, he was everything: orchestra conductor, stage director, decorator, choirmaster, and so on. Naturally, the result was something complete in itself and consistent in a way we had not heard before." Obviously, Mahler's indirect successor as Director of the Opera on the Ring, Herbert von Karajan, in demanding uniting musical and theatrical leadership in one hand, had modeled himself on his predecessor.

Mahler's Brief Career as Subscription Concert Conductor

Even Hans Richter had to yield to Mahler's drive for power: after almost 200 Philharmonic concerts, he stood at the orchestra podium on March 27, 1898, for the last time, before leaving, officially for reasons of health. The new Court Opera Director was elected to be his successor. A judgment Richter gave years later, likely coined for Mahler and his "un-Viennese" fanatic precision: "Drill sergeants belong on the parade ground."

Mahler led a Philharmonic subscription concert for the first time on November 6, 1898, but what could have been the beginning of a splendid collaboration came to an end not much later. In January 1902, with a performance of his Fourth Symphony, he bade the organization farewell. Overwork and health problems may have led to his departure, but certainly also disputes with the orchestra, which had been subordinate to him in the Court Opera.

Hellsberg tarnishes Mahler's halo as an innovator, at least in the concert realm: One could speak of this short era as "the most conservative programming since Nicolai," for, "with Dvorak, Goldmark, Mahler and Strauss, only four living composers came to be performed"! But certainly Mahler's approach, even to old works, was new, as a review of the Beethoven Fifth shows, which was was heard on November 5, 1899: "…Fate no longer 'knocks,' it pulls down the gates. And this is no mere assault, but an invasion into a new world of feeling—Beethoven, not as the completion of classical development, but as the giant awakener of a new dramatic style of music." The review by Robert Hirschfeld in the *Wiener Abendpost* concludes: "We are held in fearful dramatic tension from which we are not released until the last bars."

Mahler the concert conductor did not shy away from instrumentation revisions in Beethoven's Symphonies. For this, he had to take not just the reproof of critics at home, but also the posthumous objections of a colleague. When Mahler became the chief conductor of the New York Philharmonic after leaving Vienna, he "exported" his interventions and noted on the first page of the conductor's score of Beethoven's Seventh Symphony in blue pencil: "Changes by G. Mahler." And aggressively scribbled underneath (in English) we find a judgment on these changes: "Unworthy of such a musician. A. Toscanini."

Mahler was the first leader of the Philharmonic concerts who was not also the Chairman of the orchestra. In place of the overly busy opera director, bassist Simandl was named the first "Obmann" from the ranks of the orchestra. He was succeeded by flutist Alois Markl, who served from 1903 to 1923, thus even after he retired.

One high point in the history of the orchestra was its first trip abroad under the direction of Gustav Mahler: it brought the Philharmonic to the Paris World Exposition in June 1900. But insufficient publicity and correspondingly low attendance at the concerts led to a financial debacle that Mahler could only avoid because he managed to wrest coverage of the deficit from Baron Albert Rothschild. During said trip, the orchestra and its conductor became closer again, but this reconciliation was not to last.

When Mahler resigned the leadership of the Philharmonic Subscription Concerts in 1901, Bruno Walter, who had just debuted at the opera in April of that year, was considering his own chances at succeeding Mahler. But instead of him, "they took Hellmesberger, a master shoemaker of the first rank," wrote Walter to his father indignantly.

Hellmesberger's Resignation

Joseph Hellmesberger was not destined to lead the Philharmonic Concerts for long, either. The son of Georg Hellmesberger was also his successor as concertmaster, and had been successful as a conservatory teacher, ballet conductor, and as a composer of over 20 operettas, but was attested to be only "mediocre" as the new Philharmonic conductor. Clemens Hellsberg's judgment of this all-too-busy man was as follows: "Anyone who switches between Beethoven's Ninth in the context of the Nicolai-Concert to leading the *Veilchenmädel* in the Carltheater could likely not be compared to Richter or Mahler."

Although he was a favorite of the ladies, the public thrashing Hellmesberger (Joseph, aka "the handsome Pepi") got at the hands of the father of a ballet dancer he was involved with turned out to have fateful consequences. His resignation in September 1903, right before the season began, led the Philharmonic to try working with guest conductors

Gustav Mahler (center) and his orchestra: memorial tablet of the Paris tour of 1900

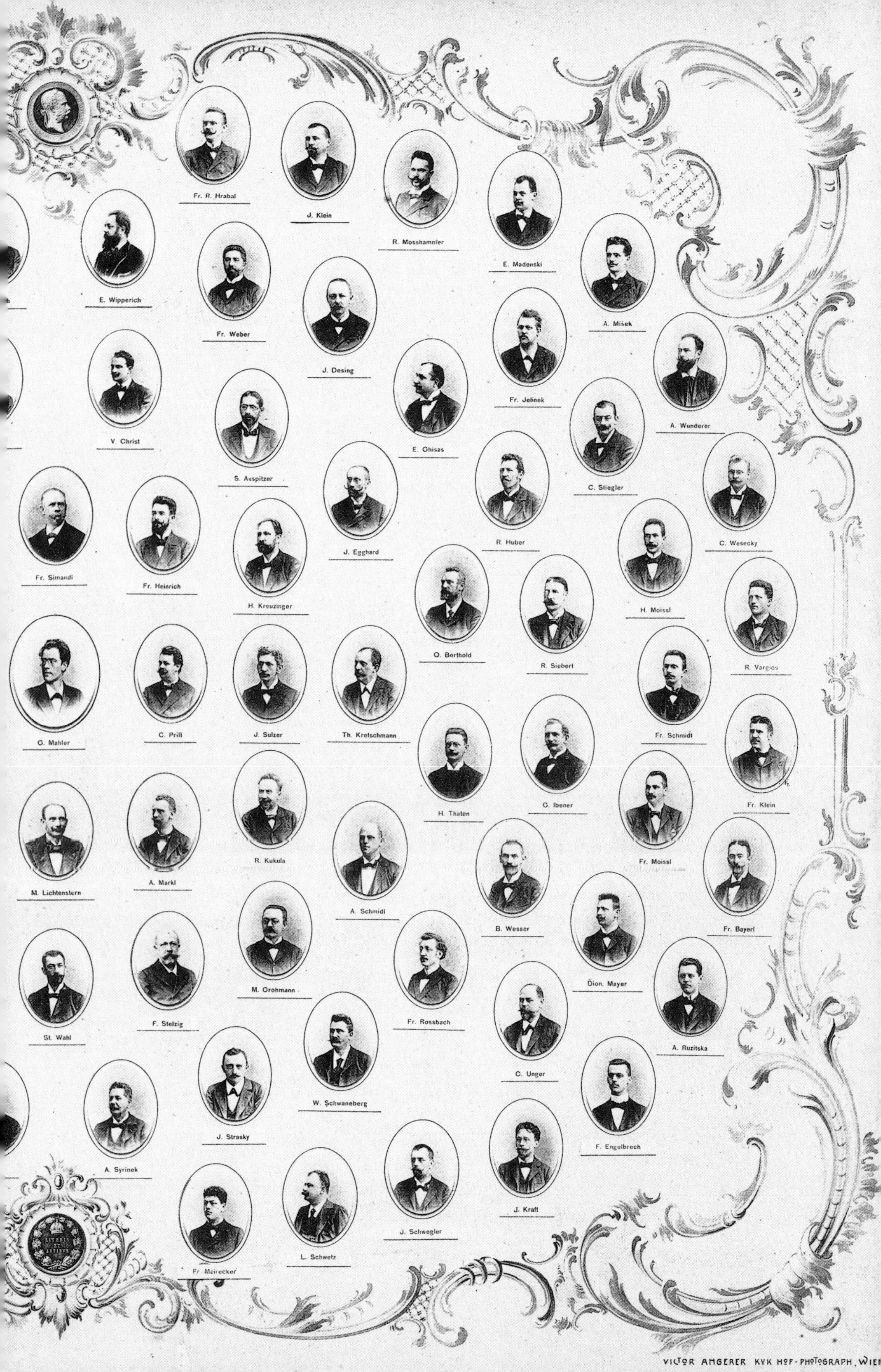
Fr. R. Hrabal
J. Klein
R. Mosshammer
E. Madenski
E. Wipperich
Fr. Weber
J. Desing
A. Mišek
Fr. Jelinek
V. Christ
S. Auspitzer
E. Ghisas
A. Wunderer
C. Stiegler
J. Egghard
R Huber
C. Wesecky
Fr. Simandl
Fr. Heinrich
H. Kreuzinger
O. Berthold
H. Moissl
R. Siebert
R. Vargics
G. Mahler
C. Prill
J. Sulzer
Th. Kretschmann
Fr. Schmidt
H. Thaten
G. Ibener
Fr. Klein
M. Lichtenstern
A. Markl
R. Kukula
Fr. Moissl
A. Schmidl
B. Wesser
Fr. Bayerl
M. Grohmann
Dion. Mayer
St. Wahl
F. Stelzig
Fr. Rossbach
A. Ruzitska
W. Schwaneberg
C. Unger
J. Strasky
A. Syrinek
F. Engelbrech
J. Kraft
J. Schwegler
L. Schwetz
Fr. Meirecker
VICTOR ANGERER K.u.K. HOF-PHOTOGRAPH. WIEN

(a system that would not become permanent until 1933). Before we examine this short phase of the orchestra's history, though, let us turn again to Mahler.

Anti-Semitism?

Without doubt Gustav Mahler also had to struggle with resentment that was motivated by anti-Semitism. In order to get the job of director, however, he had been willing to convert to Christianity. Arnold Rosé had taken this step before him and had also changed his name (originally Rosenblum).

But here we encounter some contradictory facts. At that time, in this "multi-ethnic orchestra" (Merlin), there were just 18% Jews, who were in no way unanimously inclined to be pro Mahler, although the rejection of Mahler was mainly as a composer. The legendary solo cellist Joseph Sulzer, for instance, the son of the Viennese cantor Salomon Sulzer, flatly rejected the work of the Court Opera director. "Who is this composer Mahler? No one knows him," opined Sulzer in a committee session in April 1899—at this time, the first two symphonies of this "unknown" had already had their world premieres! The Jewish cellist Theobald Kretschmann wrote in 1913, thus, two years after Mahler's death, that he "admired him as a finely sensitive Mozart conductor and an extraordinary worker with enormous ability." But it troubled Kretschmann "to see him lost in these compositional aberrations that completely misrepresented him; I was greatly shocked to see these aberrations being applauded and to see him reinforced in his errors!" Merlin confirms this: "the partisanship for or against Mahler did not always follow the usual lines of conflict."

This is also shown by the following episode: When the Vienna City Council appealed to the Philharmonic for their support at a festival concert to aid the poor of Vienna, only Mahler was considered as a conductor. But he was rejected by the openly anti-Semitic city government under Mayor Karl Lueger. The orchestra persisted in supporting their own elected conductor, and the concert was cancelled.

While the Jewish ancestry of the Philharmonic conductor Otto Dessoff had never been an issue, with the beginning of the new century, the opposing fronts hardened steadily, both in Viennese society as well as within the orchestra. In 1907, Mahler, unnerved by (sometimes anti-Semitic) hostilities, disappointed in his fellow men and in failing health, left Vienna and the Court Opera. His relationship with the Philharmonic was very tense for long periods, but for his artistic verdict, a statement he made to Alois Markl in June 1903 suffices: that he, who "has been able to hear all the significant orchestras of the world," returns to Vienna again and again, "convinced that our orchestra far surpasses all the others."

The First Guest Conductor Phase

All the Philharmonic conductors of the first 60 years (with the exception of the stand-in Hellmesberger and the guest conductor Siegfried Wagner, the composer's son, who was made an honorary conductor of a Nicolai concert in 1896) had also been conductors (Kapellmeister) of the Court Opera. In the fall of 1903, to save their concert season (Hellmesberger had resigned in September 1903, only weeks before the beginning of the season), the Philharmonic sought prominent conductors and at first found, significantly, two students of Otto Dessoff: Arthur Nikisch, who had been the first violinist from 1874 to 1877, and the Graz native Ernst von Schuch, who rendered outstanding service with the operas of Richard Strauss particularly in Dresden.

Even Maestro Strauss himself was persuaded to help with the concerts: in 1906, he began an almost 40-year collaboration with the orchestra. Court Opera conductor Franz Schalk was called back several times—"Together with Richard Strauss, he led a Philharmonic season and in doing so offered the Concert hall foretaste of the future joint directorship Strauss/Schalk in the Vienna State Opera" (Blaukopf)—the loyal Schalk, even then, had to accept the fact that he was only the second choice for the Philharmonic and was welcomed more as a stand-in.

A few prominent names among the subscription directors of those years: Felix Mottl, a former student of the Vienna Conservatory, who brought new compositions of Hans Pfitzner, Max von Schillings, Edward Elgar, and especially Richard Strauss' *Ein Heldenleben* to the program; Karl Muck, who first performed Bruckner's Ninth as part of the Nicolai Concerts of 1906; Bruno Walter, who finally made his Philharmonic debut at the Nicolai Concerts of 1907.

In that year, a new Director for the Court Opera was appointed as well: Felix Weingartner. The choice at the orchestra's general meeting in May 1908 fell upon him, who had never yet conducted the Vienna Philharmonic, but was entrusted with leading the subscription concerts beginning with the 1908/09 season. With this, the principle of a fixed subscription concert conductor in the person of the opera director again won the upper hand.

One judgment from Julius Korngold, Eduard Hanslick's successor at the *Neue Freie Presse* (and father of the prodigy composer Erich Wolfgang Korngold), shows the critical opposition to the idea of alternating conductors as the century began. They could be harmful to the identity of the Philharmonic Orchestra, "because it is nourished by a distinct character that must not be endangered."

The Weingartner Era

The "year of change" 1908 saw not only the return to the system of a permanent subscription conductor, but also the founding of the Vienna Philharmonic Association, the purpose of which was to provide for the sick and aging members of the orchestra. This organizational form is still valid within our orchestra today.

The Weingartner era lasted until 1927. The "Big Three" in the annals of our institution were (sorted by number of concerts and also by length of tenure) Hans Richter (193 subscription concerts, 22 years), Felix Weingartner (156, 19 years), and Otto Dessoff (129, 15 years). But if you include the tours, non-subscription concerts and the open (as of 1917) dress rehearsals of the orchestra under Weingartner's direction, he is clearly the most active conductor of the Philharmonic. As Karl Böhm attested of his older colleague: "He was the ideal conductor for the orchestra musicians. His markings were simple; his gestures practical, yet not just beating the time, but appropriate to the phrase and the expression"…Böhm also described his own conducting this way!

It was also during Weingartner's era that the Philharmonic assisted in the first Vienna Music Festival Weeks (1912), which would become

Arnold Schönberg was an infrequent guest conductor of the orchestra…

…Felix Weingartner, on the other hand, was the Philharmonic conductor most often at the podium.

the Vienna Festival Weeks, and in that same year, the posthumous world premiere of Gustav Mahler's Ninth Symphony took place under the direction of the "Mahler apostle" Bruno Walter. But the Salzburg Festival of 1914 could not take place: the First World War was raging throughout Europe, 26 Philharmonic members had to join up, and the trumpet player Adolf Wunderer (brother of the later Chairman Alexander Wunderer) died in action.

One of their rare trips abroad took them to neutral Switzerland, where the 'Zauberorchester' ("magical orchestra") was acclaimed in a Swiss newspaper with these optimistic words: "It has been granted us to see the day when even those who still call themselves enemies will enthusiastically hail the highest artistic culture, which comes to us from Austria with the Philharmonic."

The immediate post-war period shows us an orchestra no less active in opera and concert programs. Of the many high points we shall emphasize only one, the meeting with Arnold Schönberg. He conducted two performances of his *Gurrelieder* in 1920 and outdid himself in a written panegyric to the orchestra: "the select, the elect few of art, such as you, gentlemen, make also those who are themselves gladly chosen, to be their elector, and so let me write on my electoral ballot: The Vienna Philharmonic."

After the First World War, Weingartner was almost to become the generalissimo of Viennese musical life, for he was considered the leader of both the *Staatsoper* and the *Volksoper* for a time. But eventually he had to be "content" with the *Volksoper* while his rival Richard Strauss got the position in the larger house. Nonetheless he would go down in history books as a two time Director of the *Staatsoper* (1907–11, and 1935/36) as well as Director of the *Volksoper* (1919–24).

South America, Times Two

Weingartner took the orchestra on its first South American tour from mid-June to mid-September of 1922. Co-director Franz Schalk of the State Opera put together a lighter playing schedule that could be handled by a "rump orchestra."

Alexander Witeschnik recounts the infantile delight of the Philharmonic musicians in "discovering" the equator: "As the orchestra neared the equator on its first South American tour, the entire crew went into Carnival mode. The champagne corks were popping, there was an extravagant festive meal and a musical variety program in which Jacques van Lier and Friedrich Buxbaum were master comedians [...] April Fool's jokes made the rounds. One travel-weary colleague was reassured: 'Be glad when the ship crosses the equator, then we will be going much faster, because it's downhill from there.' Another timid member was advised, 'Hide all your cigarettes, they have very strict luggage inspection at the equator!' The biggest attraction was trying the see the equator with binoculars. One clever Philharmonic member had inserted a piece of thread behind the lens of his field glasses; he handed them round to anyone who was interested, and, look, the zero-latitude line was plain to see. So this is how the Vienna Philharmonic discovered the equator."

Felix Weingartner describes more serious travel impressions in his autobiography: "I had a strangely joyous sensation as I was driving to my hotel when I saw an advertisement in the streets of this tropical city, announcing in giant letters, 'The Vienna Philharmonic.' An excited audience filled the Teatro Municipal to the last seat, the numerous stately looking, noble-profiled members of the orchestra, which despite the suffering of the war had maintained their dignified bearing, had a surprising, evocative effect even before the first note was played. We were able to celebrate a series of artistic festivals that fulfilled my hopes for the trip." One of Weingartner's hopes, a personal re-invitation, would not be fulfilled, but more of that later.

On July 19, 1922, the Vienna Philharmonic gave its first concert outside of Europe, followed by thirty-three others as well as four opera performances (Wagner's *Ring des Nibelungen)* in the Teatro Colón. Oboist Johann Strasky found that Weingartner conducted the *Blue Danube Waltz* very quickly and addressed a coded message to him: "The Parkett (orchestra section of the audience) has very dangerous acoustics. In here, waltzes sound much too fast." Weingartner smiled, understood, and moderated his tempo for that evening's concert.

One colleague, the violist Eugen Hüttner, settled in Argentina as a violin teacher, something which violinist Daniel Falk commented on fancifully

Relaxed mood on board. Shown singing on their way to the first South American tour are Josef Geringer, Jacques van Lier, Victor Polatschek an Friedrich Buxbaum (first row)

The following year, the Philharmonic, now looking more serious, gather around conductor Richard Strauss in Rio de Janeiro.

in his diary: "Hüttner is staying in America; the plan he had made back in Vienna to work for his uncle in a factory in North America is now 'realized' by this decision. He will ride horseback with a friend from South to North America through fields and forests. Good Luck!" A proleptic historic note: Daniel Falk himself fled Nazi terror to America, and settled in New York.

The following year, the South American venture was repeated, but, at the request of the organizers, with a new conductor. Opera director Richard Strauss, of all people, Weingartner's arch-enemy, was now leading the Philharmonic—and his relationship with the orchestra was not always pleasant. This was the orchestra Mahler had "cleaned up" two and a half decades earlier. Strauss wrote to Schalk: "I have had ample opportunity during the current concerts to study the faults of our orchestra..." The next three years saw the arrival of 17 new members, which once again brought down the average age of the orchestra.

A work of Anton Bruckner was performed for the first time ever in Buenos Aires. "Was he an Austrian?" one enthusiastic visitor asked the hornist Karl Stiegler after the concert. "He was from Upper Austria, no less," he answered proudly. "You see, even our farmers compose that way."

Hugo Burghauser has another nice anecdote from the second South American tour in 1923. After 34 concerts under Richard Strauss, there was just one last appearance scheduled in Bahia, but the maestro "had already been called back by Vienna and had decided therefore to skip the last concert. He simply left while the orchestra dutifully played in an open-air arena under the Southern Cross. Alexander Wunderer acted as conductor and reaped thunderous applause as 'Ricardo Strauss' despite his goatee and bald head."

But there is more to report than just amusing anecdotes: three members of the Philharmonic did not survive the tour. Violinist Karl Knoll committed suicide, and clarinetist Franz Behrends and bassist Eduard Madensky succumbed to pneumonia.

Lifelong Friendship with Richard Strauss

Even back in 1902, four years before he conducted the orchestra, Strauss called it "the best and most beautiful sounding in Europe." After his debut with the Philharmonic at the 1906 Salzburg Mozart Festival, he played his first subscription concert on December 16 of that year with Bruckner, whom he was not particularly fond of. After several joint concerts, the composer invited the Philharmonic to the Richard-Strauss Week in Munich in June 1910, where they played *Don Juan* for the first time under the direction of its creator.

Strauss' engagement by the Vienna State Opera in 1919 did not occur without some hostility from the orchestra, but matters were soon reconciled. After the world premiere of the Vienna version of *Ariadne auf Naxos* (1916) there came another Strauss world premiere, which the composer called "one of the most glorious chapters in the history of the orchestra": *Die Frau ohne Schatten* (1919). Then came the world premieres of, among others, the *Bürger als Edelmann-Suite* (*Le bourgeois gentilhomme*) (1920) and the Ballet *Schlagobers* (*Whipped Cream*) (1924).

In 1922, the Vienna Philharmonic participated in the Salzburg Festival for the first time, whose "artists' council" included Max Reinhardt, Franz Schalk, Hugo von Hofmannsthal (author of *Jedermann*), the stage designer Alfred Roller, and—Richard Strauss. That summer he conducted performances of Mozart's *Don Giovanni* and *Così fan tutte.*

Strauss was on friendly terms with the orchestra. He also very much liked the products of hobby winemaker Franz Mairecker, whom he had pulled from the first violin section to the concertmaster's chair. Once Strauss interrupted a rehearsal with this comment to Mairecker: "Herr Konzertmeister, I am out of wine."

After his resignation as opera director (1924), Strauss remained publicly present as the most frequently performed contemporary composer and the very busiest of conductors in Vienna and Salzburg; his name is forever associated with the Vienna Philharmonic Ball as well.

The First Philharmonic Ball

The orchestra's confidence of its position, or as Chairman (since 1923) Alexander Wunderer put it, "class consciousness", would be put on public display with this initiative. The orchestra invited "members of the government, the heads of departments, the top people in the community, in art, science, finance and the citizenry to celebrate the orchestra in the feeling that its important role in society makes it the equal to all great institutions."

The first Philharmonic ball took place on March 4, 1924, in the Musikverein, of course. The *Fanfare* played at every opening to this day was a commission given to Richard Strauss, and he dedicated it to the "dear, splendid Vienna Philharmonic Orchestra members." Weingartner was enraged by this, but nonetheless conducted the most famous of all waltzes, *The Blue Danube*. The poet and two-time director of the Burgtheater Anton Wildgans composed short opening stanzas for the Ball booklet, which was given out as a party favor to the ladies. The first verse is a timeless homage to the Vienna Philharmonic:

Euch liebt die Heimat und euch ehrt die Welt!
Wann immer wir des Besten uns besinnen,
Nach dem man eines Volkes Reichtum zählt,
Da können wir getrost mit euch beginnen.
(Beloved at home, and revered by the world,
Whenever we need a measure
By which to count our nation's wealth,
To start with you is our pleasure.)

The net proceeds from the ball, 60 million crowns (in the new currency just introduced a few days before the ball, 6000 schillings, roughly double the annual salary of an orchestra musician), were deposited into the Nicolai pension fund. The Philharmonic Ball existed until 1931, at which event Strauss personally conducted the world premiere of his orchestral piece *Kampf und Sieg*, until the worsening economic crisis made the ball financially unfeasible. The tradition was not revived again until after the Second World War.

The End of the Weingartner Era

Felix von Weingartner was considered one of the outstanding Beethoven interpreters of his time. The works of Brahms were also in his field of expertise. He was less of an advocate for Bruckner or for French or Slavic repertory. His own works, however, were frequently on his programs. To his displeasure, though, he had to concede that the public as well as the orchestra preferred the work of the late Gustav Mahler and the very much alive Richard Strauss, to his own.

New works, other than from Strauss, were not all that plentiful. In February 1925, while Weingartner still had tight control of the subscription concerts, Franz Schalk stood at the podium for the first performance of Stravinsky's *The Rite of Spring*. And scandal was not avoided here either, in part because the preparation left much to be desired.

In June/July of 1925, an extended tour of Germany took place, which, according to Hellsberg, was to "serve as propaganda for the annexation (*Anschluss*) of Austria into the Weimar Republic." And the tour was directed by, of all people, two conductors whose work in Austria would be forbidden once the *Anschluss* was carried out: Erich Kleiber and Bruno Walter. In May of 1927, Felix Weingartner bade farewell to become Conservatory and Concert Director in Basel, but continued to conduct the orchestra a number of times until 1937.

A Brief Furtwängler Era

It was Wunderer's great achievement to get one of the "greats", Wilhelm Furtwängler, as the conductor of the subscription concerts for three years (1927–29). Of course, the now "Permanent Conductor" was rather unpredictable in his scheduling arrangements and was also the chief conductor of the Berlin Philharmonic "on the side", which made it a good thing to have Franz Schalk as "co-conductor" to fall back on when needed. After Richard Strauss' departure, Schalk led the Vienna State Opera alone until 1929. When he was appointed *Generalmusikdirektor*, he opined: "As far as I am concerned, you can drop the 'General', maybe then there would be more music left." His famous last words from 1931, "Take care of my

e Philharmonic with
nz Schalk in Salzburg
28)

ways on the move:
e very busy Wilhelm
rtwängler at the train
ation

Opera director and
last chief conductor of
the Vienna Philharmonic:
Clemens Krauss

Philharmonic musicians" ('Achtet mir auf meine Philharmoniker'), adorn the Franz Schalk Medallion. Since 1963, the Vienna Philharmonic has presented this decoration to those whose work for the orchestra has been especially meritorious.

Furtwängler rapidly distinguished himself as a favorite of the Viennese public and as an important touring conductor who took the orchestra to places such as Budapest, several German cities, and London. But plans to contract him for three more years and to make him opera director did not succeed because of resistance from his home base, Berlin.

The Last Fixed Subscription Conductor: Clemens Krauss

So an "old" solution was found. Since Weingartner's departure from the Court Opera in 1911, the offices of opera director and subscription conductor had not been in one hand. But now a new State Opera director was "discovered:" young Clemens Krauss (only 36), who had first conducted the Philharmonic in 1924. He was a former star student at the Vienna Conservatory and an intimate of Richard Strauss, who had helped him to get the appointment. Coming from the Frankfurt Opera, Krauss soon got himself the nickname "Frankfurtwängler". The source for this nickname, incidentally, still kept his foot in the door with the annual Nicolai Concert. With few exceptions, Furtwängler continued to conduct it until the year of his death in 1954.

With his pronounced orientation towards modern music, both in the State Opera and the Philharmonic concerts, Krauss forfeited popularity with both the public and the orchestra itself. A telling anecdote about the cellist Oskar Saubermann: at the first performance of *Wozzeck* (March 1930) led by the "host" conductor, the cellist remarked, "with this opera, they will have to give out fresh comps after the first act!"

Sales decreased at the subscription concerts, too, in part due to the world economic crisis, but unquestionably the progressive musical trend also played a role: over a third of the pieces played on the programs were contemporary works, including Debussy's *Rhapsody for Orchestra and Saxophone*, Arthur Honegger's *Pacific 231*, Schönberg's *Transfigured Night*, Berg's *Lyric Suite*, and—with no less shocking an effect than at the premiere with Schalk—*The Rite of Spring*. Neither Prokofiev nor Hindemith were to the taste of an audience that had hissed at Mahler's symphonies at the turn of the century.

Krauss drew a clear line in the sand and left Vienna to become director of the Berlin State Opera and later (1937-1944) general manager in Munich. With this he was offering himself—without ever joining the Nazi party—to the new rulers in Germany, for which Austrians did not forgive him for a long time. From 1935 to 1938, he was not invited to the Salzburg Festival and only returned to the Philharmonic when Austria had ceased to exist.

Merlin's summation sees in Krauss "one of the most courageous and modern artistic leaders of the Vienna Philharmonic." And: "it is absolutely a paradoxical situation that an orchestra which identifies itself so completely as Viennese treated its only genuinely Viennese chief conductor with the most hostility." Conversely, Krauss knew what he owed the "Viennese" players: "That the tempi and phrasings of the Brahms symphonies handed down to me through the Vienna Philharmonic Orchestra are the ones Brahms himself wanted cannot be doubted."

With the end of the brief Krauss era, Blaukopf also sees the end of the orchestra's repertorial open-mindedness: "With Krauss' departure, the Vienna Philharmonic had already exited from the music history of the twentieth century, and the aesthetic policies of the Third Reich did the rest, fixing the repertory on the old and tradition-bound."

Although the idea of a head conductor was not completely abandoned until into the 1950's, a new era began for the Vienna Philharmonic after Krauss and continues to the present day: that of the guest conductor. The architect of this new system was Hugo Burghauser.

Arturo Toscanini (center) and his orchestra. To his right Arnold Rosé, to his left (in a light jacket) Hugo Burghauser.

The Burden of History and the Dawn of a New Age

Fascism, War and Reconstruction (1933-1955)

Hugo Burghauser, bassoonist and Chairman of the Philharmonic board from 1933 to 1938, "ruled" with grand visions, and he did not shy away from brashness or going beyond his own level of competence to implement them. And so he composed a memorandum to the Ministry of Education requesting the dismissal of opera director Clemens Krauss—without authority from the orchestra.

The entry of Arturo Toscanini to the Salzburg Festival of 1934 was also at Burghauser's behest. Since at that time the orchestra was not entitled to any say in the festival's management, this arbitrary measure resulted in his temporary suspension and a disciplin hearing, until Education Minister and later Federal Chancellor Kurt Schuschnigg restored him to office.

Burghauser had earlier prevented the world premiere of Ernst Krenek's opera *Karl V.*, and so the opera did not get its Viennese premiere until 1984 at the State Opera under conductor Erich Leinsdorf—who had himself been driven out by the Nazis earlier. Burghauser thus played into the hands of the "political culture" of the brownshirt rulers of Germany. Although he, as a member of the "Vaterländische Front," stood bitterly opposed to the Nazis, he was still an exponent of the authoritarian regime which ruled Austria until 1938 and which itself had fascist characteristics.

Harbingers and Aftereffects

The years 1938 and 1945 are considered the beginning and ending points of National Socialism in Austria, but the "takeover" (*Machtergreifung*) of the National Socialists in Berlin (1933) was immediately palpable in Austria, long before the *Anschluss* in March 1938, and putting its stamp on everything, provoking either approval or opposition.

In 1933, the Nazi party was outlawed in Austria, but illegal party members such as Wilhelm Jerger and Helmut Wobisch sat side by side with Jews in the Philharmonic. From 1932 on, bassist Jerger was a Nazi party member, and after the *Anschluss* he was immediately installed as Chairman of the orchestra. Between December 1939 and May 1945, Jerger was the first and last orchestra board member who had been appointed "from above." A joke was going around about him because he had changed his Slavic surname: "Have you heard that Jerger has made a name for himself in Germany?"—"Really?"—"Yes, he used to be called Jeržabek!"

Trumpet player Wobisch also was a "high caliber" Nazi (Oliver Rathkolb), a party member since 1933 and an *Unterscharführer* in the SS since 1943. His big time in the orchestra did not come until considerably after the war. And given the surprisingly large number of former Nazis who continued to hold important positions in liberated Austria and the slow pace of rehabilitation that really didn't really get started until the 1980's, 1945 did not really represent an end point.

Some facts are worth considering, though, even if we can't interpret them as specific preliminaries for the horrors of National Socialism: the violinists Daniel Falk, Joseph Geringer, and Heinrich Schwarz (who died in 1935) had been, in September 1920, the last Jews accepted into the orchestra—with the exception of Ricardo Odnoposoff, a special case we shall discuss later. But even years before the *Anschluss,* the proportion of Jews in the orchestra had fallen to a historic low: by 1935 it was only 12%.

The fate of one individual? Clarinetist Viktor Schmidl retired in 1936 at the age of only 37, due to an eye disease. A further reason for his voluntary withdrawal may have been, "according to his son Peter, [the fact that] as a social democrat, he could no longer bear the political atmosphere in the orchestra in these years so imbued with Austro-fascism." So it is probably not far-fetched to include Schmidl among the first victims of fascism in our orchestra.

In the Musikverein in 1942: Hans Knappertsbusch, Wilhelm Jerger, Karl Böhm. On the right, hornist Leopold Kainz…

…and one more Nazi party member: Helmut Wobisch

The Maestro assoluto

The new Chair, Burghauser, knew how to turn the politics of the Nazis he despised to the orchestra's advantage. He put his stamp on the beginning era of guest conductors by inviting conductors who were not welcome in Germany, such as Bruno Walter and Otto Klemperer. The latter was only rarely invited because of his exorbitant fees, but he still paid the orchestra a special compliment: "Playing is everywhere, but making music is only in Vienna." Carl Schuricht and the 26-year-old Herbert von Karajan were two of the conductors who were new to the orchestra in the 1930's. (Karajan also debuted in 1937 at the Vienna State Opera with *Tristan und Isolde*.)

But the most spectacular debut was that of Arturo Toscanini at an "Extraordinary Philharmonic Concert" in October of 1933. Toscanini, born on March 25, 1867, and thus 25 years younger than our orchestra, almost to the day, was considered a fanatic for precision. Nonetheless, the orchestra, which normally did not like dictators on the podium, took him to their heart immediately. The Italian returned their feelings and called it "miei cari Filarmonici di Vienna che ho imparato a aprezzare e amare" ("...whom I have learned to appreciate and to love"). Salzburg, too, received its stamp from the *maestro assoluto* "as an anti-National Socialist show window. Hidden behind this praiseworthy goal, though, was another description: Hollywood on the Salzach, [...] or Salzburg as the home of stars and snobs" (Stephen Gallup).

The chronicle shows 32 Salzburg and one Vienna Opera performance (*Fidelio*) under Toscanini and 46 Philharmonic concerts conducted by him. "Since these 79 performances were connected to around 120 rehearsals, he conducted the Philharmonic about 200 times—enough to make it 'his' orchestra for those four years" (Hellsberg).

Honorary Members and Rehearsal Dodgers

In 1935, the former Philharmonic cellist Franz Schmidt led a concert dedicated to his own works only. He, along with pianist Wilhelm Backhaus, Bruno Walter, Arturo Toscanini and Richard Strauss, was made

Hans Knappertsbusch dedicated his photograph to the "Incomparable" Vienna Philharmonic in 1929.

honorary member of the orchestra. Felix Weingartner returned and did the unthinkable to an all-male orchestra: he sent his wife, the conductor Carmen Studer, to take over at a concert rehearsal in Padua, a deed which Burghauser called "terror."

Hans Knappertsbusch was also a highly esteemed conductor of that time. "Kna" was definitely not denied entry into Germany, but because of his casual attitude he was constantly having conflicts with the Nazis. He called *Parsifal* the "Bayreuth local farce", and once, when asked what he thought of a Furtwängler concert in Salzburg, he said, "good, unfortunately". His dislike of rehearsals made him dear to the hearts of the Philharmonic. He was supposed to hold a rehearsal before a concert in Düsseldorf of Bruckner's Fourth, but he opined serenely: "You know the work, I know the hall, that's enough. See you this evening!"

Burghauser not only succeeded in raising the number of non-subscription concerts in Vienna and Salzburg between 1934 and 1937 (soloist concerts with Sergei Rachmaninoff, Bronislav Huberman and Fritz Kreisler were among the high points), but also in "bringing together the artistic antipodes Toscanini and Furtwängler, the painfully precise interpreter of everything that is in the notes and the mystical discoverer of everything that is not in the notes, in one year's program" (Blaukopf).

Toscanini quits

Bruno Walter was alarmed by Furtwängler's increasingly close connection to Salzburg and the Philharmonic and wrote a letter from St. Moritz on February 4, 1938, to his "carissimo amico Toscanini." "Furtwängler's charisma is—for me, at least—politically, personally and artistically intolerable, especially in Salzburg. […] Furtwängler thinks only of one thing: himself, his fame, his success. He is a talented man with personal prestige but an evil heart, which also comes out in his music. […] in fact, what we have here is Furtwängler's intrigue against you, against me, and against the spirit of Salzburg, and we need to be aware of this and deal with it appropriately for the greater good of all" (in: Harvey Sachs).

Immediately after learning of the February 1938 "Berchtesgaden Agreement," which Hitler had forced Austrian chancellor Schuschnigg to accept—an event which led to the re-authorization of the National Socialist Party in Austria—Toscanini cancelled his participation in the Salzburg Festival. In 1934, Toscanini had shown that even a passionate democrat like him could make exceptions when he conducted Verdi's *Requiem* at the Vienna State Opera in 1934 in memory of the admittedly anti-democratic Austrian chancellor Engelbert Dollfuß, who had been murdered by the Nazis. But now the conductor stuck to his guns—and never returned to the Philharmonic desk again, not even after 1945.

The Well-prepared *Anschluss*

The Philharmonic's work as a film orchestra is one of the "continuities" which began before 1938 and lasted until after 1945. The Philharmonic violinist Franz Bartolomey remembered: "The day the German troops marched into Austria, we were ordered to the Rosenhügel film studio for a recording session—about 60 musicians from our orchestra were on the set ready to record, but no one could do any concentrated work. March music was blaring out of all the loudspeakers."

The opera director Carl Ebert described the dramatic days (March 11 and 12, 1938) of the National Socialist takeover of Austria in a letter which led to the incredulous question: "... where did all these thousands of little flags come from all of a sudden?" The overthrow—including the distribution of swastika pennants—was well prepared. Burghauser was removed from office immediately, and the "new man," Wilhelm Jerger, chose Otto Strasser as Business Manager.

Immediate Purges

Although the "Nuremberg Laws" did not take effect in Austria until May 28th, State Opera director Erwin Kerber, in anticipatory conformance, began to remove "racially" unsuitable personnel from the opera through suspension and the resulting retirement process. Since it was a statutory requirement then (and now) that only members of the State Opera Orchestra could become members of the Vienna Philharmonic, this meant exclusion from the Association as well. Merlin states "that the Philharmonic made no efforts to retain their colleagues in the Verein even temporarily, through statutory changes, for instance." Still, the only action to aid the excluded was the promise of severance pay.

After removing the nine "Volljuden" (i.e., "completely" Jewish members), management set its sights on the thirteen "Mischlinge" (i.e., of mixed parentage) and "Versippten," (i.e., married to Jewish women). Concertmaster Richard (Ricardo) Odnoposoff was a special case: born in Buenos Aires, he was considered a "foreigner without an 'Ariernachweis' (certificate of Aryan descent)." Clemens Krauss put him in the State Opera as concertmaster without an audition. But since he was unable to produce "certification of Aryan descent in Russia, despite every effort," the young virtuoso, in mutual agreement with the orchestra, had to leave. He began an international solo career and was succeeded by Willi Boskovsky. In 1956, he returned to Vienna as a teacher at the Music Academy. (Not until the present century would the State Opera get another concertmaster with South American roots (the Brazilian-German violinist José Maria Blumenschein succeeded Rainer Küchl on September 1, 2016.)

The Furtwängler List

In August of 1938, Wilhelm Furtwängler wrote a letter to State Opera director Kerber (also known as the "Furtwängler List") petitioning for the "continuance" of nine musicians. On this list was Hugo Burghauser, whom Jerger had already threatened with confinement to Dachau on March 12; he divorced his wife, the Jewish ballet mistress and director Margarethe Wallmann, later in 1938. Further names on the list: the violinist Theodor Hess, hornist Gottfried Freiberg, trombonist Josef Hadraba, clarinetist Rudolf Jettel, cellists Richard Krotschak (solo) and Karl Maurer, and the solo violists Ernst Morawec and Otto Rieger. The violist Erich Weis, violinist Leopold Föderl, and timpanist Arthur Schurig, although "volljüdisch-versippt" and therefore also endangered, were not on the list. Although a "Mischling" himself, Weis stayed in the orchestra thanks to a close Nazi party connection. Schurig was banned professionally but could make do with substituting in the orchestra. Föderl's exclusion from the list "may have been a case of intrigue and harassment" (Mayrhofer). But even those who remained in the orchestra owing to "special permits" were under permanent pressure and were "in any case far removed from having equal status [...] with the rest of the Philharmonic" (Mayrhofer).

Without trying to retrace all the measures taken by the "bureaucracy of expulsion" and recount the details of all the personal martyrdoms here, (Mayrhofer and Trümpi's book *Orchestrierte Vertreibung* has done this well), the fates of the persecuted should be highlighted here.

The Murdered

Two people who died in Vienna should also be considered victims of the violence: Anton Weiss died of a stroke in 1940 at the age of 64 after several forced evictions. Paul Fischer had to agree to a compulsory retirement with a greatly reduced pension after 39 years of service, was evicted and became seriously ill. He died at 66 in the Jewish Hospital in Malzgasse. His "untended gravesite in the Kahlenberg Cemetery was discovered [years later] by accident by a retired member of the Vienna Philharmonic [Horst Münster] and [...] since then has been tended to by order of the orchestra" (Mayrhofer).

In October, Wilhelm Jerger attempted to prevent the deportation of five Jewish colleagues to a concentration camp with a letter to the Generalreferent Walter Thomas, an advisor to Reichsstatthalter Baldur von Schirach (see illustration, following page). The attempt failed—all five became victims of the Holocaust.

Moriz Glattauer was pensioned, evicted, moved to a "Jewish group home," and finally ended up in Theresienstadt, where the 73-year old died in 1943. His wife Anna was murdered the following year in Auschwitz.

After four forced evictions, the married couple Viktor and Elsa Robitsek were deported to Łodz, where they died a year later.

Max Starkmann, who was forced into retirement after 27 years of service, made an attempt to find employment with the orchestra of the Stockholm Opera—the application was rejected. In his case, also after several evictions, he was deported with his wife Elsa in a mass transport. They were executed immediately after their arrival in the extermination camp of Maly Trostinec in October 1942.

Concertmaster Julius Stwertka, brought from Hamburg to the Vienna State Opera back in 1902 by Gustav Mahler, had retired by 1938. The influential teacher (the exiled violinists Daniel Falk and Josef Geringer were among his students) was also evicted several times and deported to Theresienstadt in 1942, where he played with a string quartet for "recreation." He died that same year, and his wife and both children died in Auschwitz.

Oboist Armin Tyroler, also originally brought on by Mahler, was a highly respected person. He was the first member of the orchestra to be awarded

23.Oktober 41.

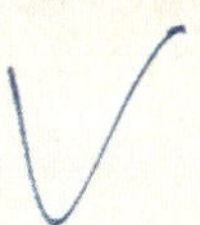

Herrn Generalreferenten
Walter T h o m a s ,
W i e n I.
Ballhausplatz 2.

Herr Generalreferent,

zu meinem Bedauern muß ich nochmals mit einer Bitte zu Ihnen kommen.

Es handelt sich um 5 ehemalige jüdische Mitglieder, die fast ein Menschenalter der Staatsoper und den Philharmonikern angehört haben. Ich würde bitten, in Anbetracht der langjährigen Verdienste - Tyroler war lange Zeit Leitungsmitglied der Philharmoniker und bekam seinerzeit den Ehrenring der Gemeinde Wien, Stvertka war bis zu seiner Pensionierung im Jahre 1937 Konzertmeister der Staatsoper und der Philharmoniker, sowie Professor an der Akademie. Eine Reihe von Geigern im Orchester sind seine Schüler.

Ich wäre Ihnen dankbar, wenn sich, was diese 5 alten Mitglieder betrifft, eine Regelung in der Frage der Verschikkung in die Wege leiten ließe und gebe Ihnen nachstehend die Namen bekannt:

68 Armin Israel Tyroler, IX., Georg Sigelgasse 9/8
64 1/2 Viktor Israel Robitschek,Pension Zenz,VIII.,Alserstr.21.
(54) 61 Max Israel Starkmann, II., Rembrandtstrasse 6/7
71 Moritz Israel Glattauer, I.,Annagasse 3 I.St.
69 Julius Israel Stwertka, III., Udetgasse 4.

Heil Hitler!

Ihr

sehr ergebener

Jerger

Chair Wilhelm Jerger's futile attempt to save colleagues from concentration camps

uno Walter and Anton
eiss (center: unknown)

Moriz Glattauer

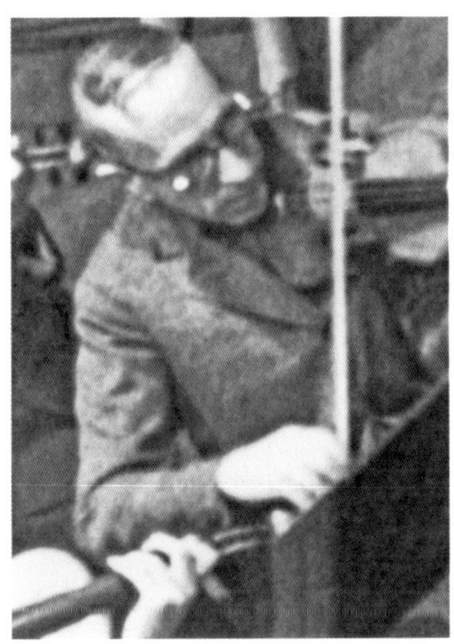

Viktor Robitsek,
below: Julius
Stwertka

Armin Tyroler

the honorary ring of the city of Vienna for his social contributions. In 1938, he provided "essential financial help for the flight of his daughter and her family" (Trümpi) from Vienna; but Tyroler could not save himself. He was deported to Theresienstadt together with Stwertka, where he continued to play music until he was brought to Auschwitz at the age of 71, where he was gassed in 1944.

The Exiles

Eight members of the Philharmonic—in addition to Odnoposoff—were able to save their own lives by fleeing. After undergoing degrading and financially very burdensome procedures, the "emigrants" were faced with an insecure position in the lands they arrived in, where refugees were in no way always met with open arms. Switzerland regarded itself merely as a 'transit' country (at the instigation of the Swiss government, the notorious "J-Stamp" was introduced to identify the passports of German Jews), in Great Britain there was a general work ban for immigrating musicians, and in the USA they were blocked from work for half a year.

Hugo Burghauser fled via Budapest, Zagreb, Milan (where he took shelter with Toscanini) and Paris to New York. There he put the full force of his artistic and political personality at the service of various political exiles' bourgeois/conservative organizations, such as "Austrian Action," and made music with the exiled violinists Ludwig Wittels, Berthold Salander and Josef Geringer in the group they founded, "the Salzburg Players." Their exiles' motto, "Hitler's First Victim Fights for Freedom," was misused after the war, by those who had stayed in Austria as a defense. Burghauser worked as a musician and teacher in Toronto and, owing to his connections with Toscanini, got a job with his NBC Symphony Orchestra in New York, and finally, from 1943 to his retirement in 1965, he was a member of the Metropolitan Opera Orchestra.

Thanks to support from the German-American banker Gerald F. Warburg, Salander was able to leave Austria with one of the last refugee transports in May 1941. But he was not able to establish himself in his New York exile, was chronically ill and died in 1959. Daniel Falk, Geringer and Wittels, at any rate, got positions in the Metropolitan Opera. Regarding the

A picture from better times: Hugo Burghauser's and Margarethe Wallmann's wedding

former violin prodigy Wittels, the aftereffects of an early childhood illness developed into a fatal condition, making him completely unable to work until he died in 1956. Falk, who had written down his "travel destination" as "all the cities of the world" on his emigration application, and Geringer both died at a ripe old age in New York. Geringer managed to escape the horrors of the concentration camp: his friendship with Jerger (the Nazi Orchestra Chair), of all people, under whom he had played several times, resulted in Jerger arranging his release from Dachau in 1939, thus saving his life.

The Figureheads: Buxbaum and Rosé

Two "figureheads" (Merlin) of the orchestra were the first to be removed in 1938. The nearly 70-year-old solo cellist Friedrich Buxbaum fled to London in the fall of 1938, and the long-time concertmaster Arnold Rosé followed, by now 75 years old, in 1939. Not until the re-establishment of the Rosé Quartet with the support of Sir Adrian Boult were they able to find musical support. On weekdays they played the "Lunchtime Concerts" at the National Gallery and also at performances to benefit exiles at the 100-year jubilee of the Philharmonic in the spring of 1942.

After 56 years of quartet playing and 44 years in the Hofmusikkapelle, Rosé, concertmaster of the Court and the State Opera since 1881, had sunk into retirement, "*ohne Sang und Klang*", as he wrote to his friend violinist Carl Flesch. He was made an honorary member of the Philharmonic as late as 1935, but now his supposed friend Richard Strauss was pulling away, and Rosé's wife Justine passed away in August 1938. Supported financially by Toscanini and Bruno Walter, he could keep himself above water until the new quartet performances gave him a new lease on life. Rosé died in 1946 in London. He lived long enough to hear of the murders of Starkmann, Robitsek and especially his daughter Alma a year and a half after she had died in Auschwitz-Birkenau. "Buxbaum also told him that an overwhelming majority of National Socialists could still be active in the Society of the Vienna Philharmonic" (Mayrhofer).

Buxbaum also lived to see the Philharmonic's guest tour of England under Bruno Walter in September 1947. "The goal of this tour of good will was to improve the reputation of Austria [...] and for the Philharmonic to rehabilitate itself internationally" (Mayrhofer). Walter used the often cited words about the "world history" which the Philharmonic had made with this tour, and even the Jewish Buxbaum could once again take his old seat in the orchestra, to which the Chair Alfred Boskovsky kindly invited him. Burghauser passed down the words which "Bux" used as he sat down with his old colleagues: "I heard you tuning up. It sounded flawless. Totally *Jew-less*!

In the following year, Wilhelm Furtwängler led the London tour of the orchestra. (Mayrhofer: "after the expiration of his professional ban in November 1947 he once again occupied his sacrosanct position as

The Rosé Quartet: Paul Fischer, Arnold Rosé, Friedrich Buxbaum, Anton Ruzitska

Rosé with Max Starkmann and Josef Geringer

conductor—and especially as tour conductor of the Vienna Philharmonic.") But he countermanded the offer that had been made to Buxbaum to play with the orchestra again: the aging (79-year-old) cellist was having tremors. Deeply hurt by Furtwängler's judgment that he was "a fault in the beautiful fabric of this splendid orchestra," Buxbaum succumbed to a heart attack the next day. However, the orchestra could not bring itself to issue pension payments to his widow until six years later.

"Special Cases": Föderl and Jettel

Rudolf Jettel, a janitor's son who had worked his way up from playing in popular bands to be a solo clarinetist in the Philharmonic as well as a composer and esteemed teacher of a generation of musicians, was on Furtwängler's List and was allowed to continue in his position even though he was married to a Jew. "What do I care about the war? Fuck the war!" Rudolf Jettel said this publicly in September of 1939 when their salaries were reduced to aid the "Winterhilfe Danzig" (charity to aid families of soldiers). The percussionist Georg Raimund and the hornist Leopold Kainz (founder of the "Betriebszelle Oper", a meeting place for illegal Nazis, and now Chairman of the opera orchestra) denounced Jettel to opera director Kerber, who immediately suspended the "culprit". After a few days, Jettel was brought back into the orchestra, for Furtwängler insisted on having him play in Richard Strauss' *Till Eulenspiegel.*

For the rest of his Philharmonic career, Jettel kept his distance from the colleagues that had nearly cost him his existence. Still, he never regretted rejecting an offer made to him in the mid-30's: "Radio Waltz King" Marek Weber invited him to play popular music with the NBC Orchestra. When Jettel and Weber met each other after the war, the conductor said: "My saxophonist got filthy rich!" The musician answered: "Alexander Girardi once said, you can't eat dumplings made of gold. And I agree with him."

The equally brilliant violinist Leopold Föderl, on the other hand, was not on Furtwängler's saving list and was suspended even before the *Anschluss.* Burghauser had accused him of being a "nihilist" and an "anarchist" because he had protested about an overly long rehearsal under Furtwängler. His "direct approach and his liberal political attitude" (Mayrhofer) made him unacceptable both for the Austrofascists and for the Nazis. Föderl fled and became a conductor and teacher in Chicago. But his return after 1945 was made difficult for him while "a quite significant number of the 'colleagues' who had driven me from my homeland are still enjoying their old exalted positions," as Föderl wrote in a letter in 1947. In the same year, the hopes he had of being offered conductorship of the State Opera in Vienna were dashed by director Franz Salmhofer. In 1954, Föderl settled as a violin teacher at the Music Academy in Vienna, where he died in 1959.

Re-Orientation

The final tally of victims is devastating: 17 Philharmonic players, 13 active and 4 retired, became victims of the regime. Nine went into exile, five were murdered in concentration camps, two died in Vienna, and one stayed here. Not just the purges were carried out quickly, but the general re-orientation towards Nazi Germany as well: the orchestra traveled to Berlin with Wilhelm Furtwängler in April 1938, they kicked out Artur Rodzinski and gave Knappertsbusch the subscription concert in May, they played concerts under Richard Strauss, who had enthusiastically jumped in for Bruno Walter and Arturo Toscanini. Back again playing under Furtwängler, the "Viennese" made a guest appearance at the Nazi party rally in Nuremberg with *Meistersinger*—Adolf Hitler was visibly thrilled.

The Philharmonic's fears of a dissolution of the *Verein* (its quasi-insurance company-like composition was now illegal) were quickly dispelled in December 1938; it was a harder fight to retain independence in the choice of a conductor, as this issue was a thorn in Joseph Goebbels' side. The domineering Furtwängler proved to be helpful here, too, just as did the new *Reichsstatthalter* (governor) of Vienna as of 1940, Baldur von Schirach. A change to the charter was ordered, and the purpose of the association was now "to preserve orchestral music at its highest perfection." Jerger authorized this programmatic reversion: it was the orchestra's duty not "to promote contemporaries, but to perform the best and most beautiful of the entire orchestral literature in consummate form"—and it remains that today.

Conductor Continuity

During the time Austria was part of the "Thousand Year Reich," there were 57 Philharmonic concerts. Looking beyond 1945, one sees an astonishing continuity of conductors. Furtwängler, chief conductor of the Berlin and from 1940 "permanent conductor" of the Vienna Philharmonic, was the most frequently employed with 55 subscription concerts from 1938 to 1954, followed by Knappertsbusch (28), who conducted at least one concert per season until 1963. Krauss did not come back to the subscription concerts until 1944 (the reconciliation lasted ten years!) and conducted 16 times after his professional ban expired (1947) until his death (1954). Karl Böhm, whom Furtwängler accepted, conducted 12, and Karajan, whom Furtwängler hated, four subscription concerts starting with his debut in January 1946. In March, however, the "implicated" Karajan was banned from conducting and one Philharmonic concert had to be cancelled a few hours before the dress rehearsal.

At one Musikverein concert of Furtwängler's after the lifting of his ban in November 1947, there was a melee at which the Russian sentry in front of the Hotel Imperial gave off a warning shot. The hall, filled with political activists, was cleared and the concert took place after an hour's delay.

There was a break with Karajan in 1950, when Furtwängler, who had ceded Bach's *St. Matthew Passion* to him, reclaimed it for himself after Karajan assumed the rehearsals. Furtwängler threatened (not for the first time) never to conduct in Vienna again, at which point the Philharmonic dropped Karajan. He would not conduct the orchestra again for six years.

Despite the political upheavals, the years from 1938 to 1954 can be seen as a unit of orchestral history: the Furtwängler Era. The other conductors mentioned, who all more or less had a close relationship to the Nazi regime, survived the changing times at the Philharmonic podium. Böhm, the last State Opera director of the Nazi period, also became the first director of the house in liberated Austria. It fell to him to conduct Beethoven's *Fidelio* on November 5, 1955, in the newly rebuilt Opera house.

The Nazi sympathizer Willem Mengelberg was also invited to conduct subscription concerts several times in the 1930's. The Philharmonic members called him "Bemängelberg" because he would talk down to them like a schoolteacher. ["Bemängeln" means "find fault with"]. Thus, he instructed clarinetist Leopold Wlach not to stand his instrument up vertically on his knee, but to lay it horizontally on his lap. The self-assured Wlach (who was on the list of "irreplaceables" after 1945) did not let this pass without comment: "Maestro, I don't tell you how you should hold your stick when your are *not* conducting, either."

The Centennial Celebration

The founding of our orchestra by Nicolai in 1842 was celebrated in a four-week-long festival with no fewer than 12 concerts. Böhm, Knappertsbusch, Strauss, Krauss and of course Furtwängler conducted, the latter giving a legendary speech in the Musikverein on March 28. His words are often quoted: "If an American orchestra demonstrates what in the highest sense can be had for money, for a great deal of money, then our Philharmonic musicians are something—just the way they are—that could not be created, hired, or replaced, by all the money in the world."

Furtwängler's statement thus denied "American" orchestras tradition (the New York Philharmonic was also founded in 1842!) and the Viennese high salaries, but this is not as important as his opposition to any idea of putting the Vienna Philharmonic under state control (as had happened with the Berlin Philharmonic): "In the new Germany in particular, we need to be aware of what an incomparable treasure the Vienna Philharmonic represents and that with it we have also taken on the obligation to protect this asset and allow it to continue to be effective."

Out of perhaps understandable gratitude, Baldur von Schirach was presented with the Vienna Philharmonic honorary ring. Less understandably, however, after Schirach was released from imprisonment for war crimes twenty-five years later, a delegate from the Philharmonic presented him with a duplicate of the ring! We can no longer determine whose idea this was: in any case, it remains a stain of dishonor in the post-war history of the orchestra.

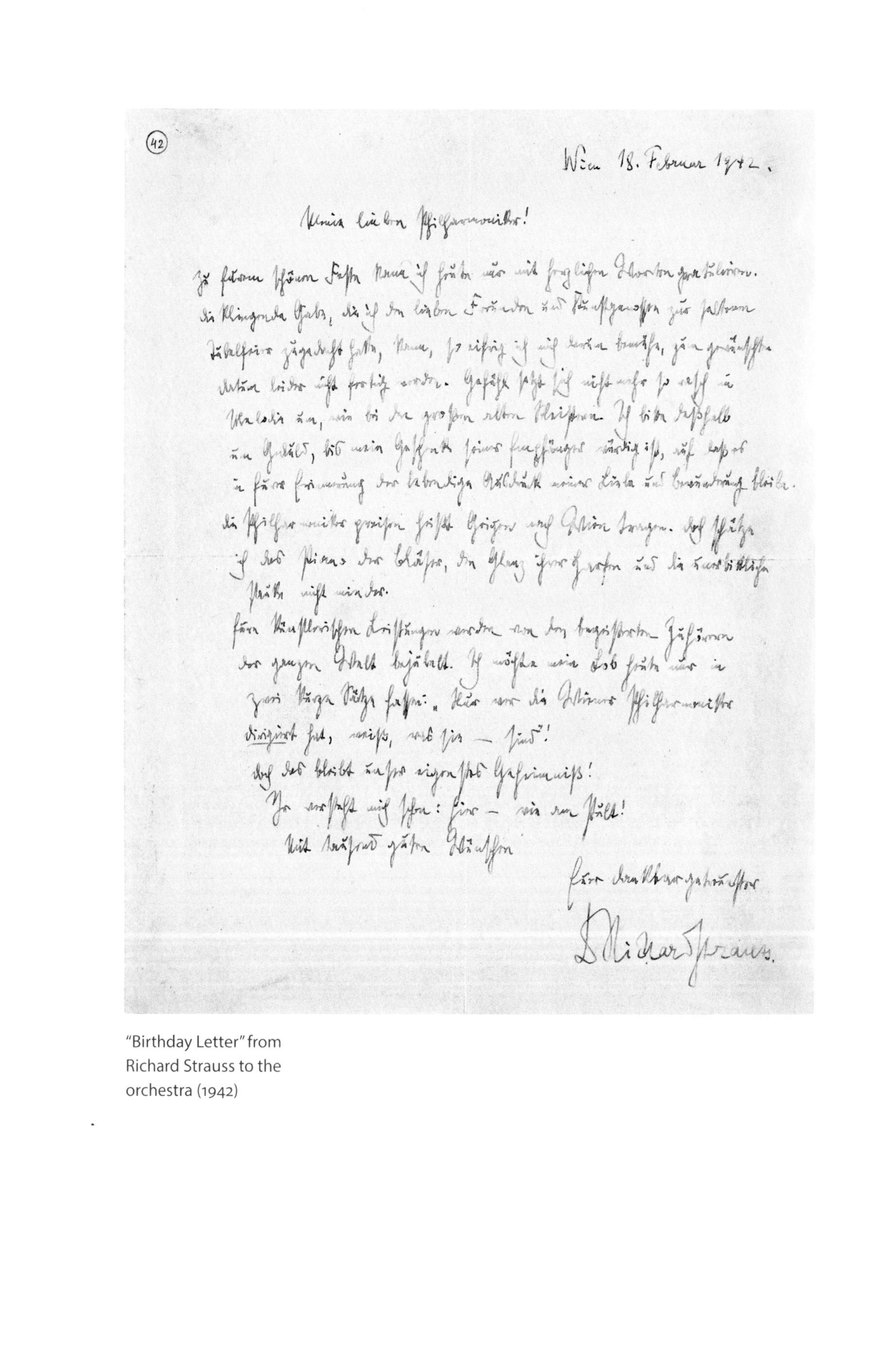

42

Wien 18. Februar 1942.

Meine lieben Philharmoniker!

[illegible]

Dr. Richard Strauss.

"Birthday Letter" from Richard Strauss to the orchestra (1942)

Birthday party for Richard Strauss (1939): the maestro sitting between daughter-in-law Alice and wife Pauline, next to them are son Franz and grandson Christian.

It can be seen as an act of subversion (or maybe just a slip-up?) that a history of the orchestra written in 1942 gave a count of the "non-Aryan" members without identifying them; it was only "corrected" after going to the press with an "erratum" slip. In the end, the book was suppressed.

Farewell to Strauss and Pfitzner

Richard Strauss sent a friendly "Birthday Letter" to the orchestra: "[…] praising the Philharmonic is like carrying violins to Vienna [tr: roughly, coals to Newcastle]. But I cherish the brass instruments' *piano*, the sheen of the harps and the implacable timpani no less. […] I should like to express my praise in two short sentences: Only a person who has *conducted* the musicians of the Vienna Philharmonic knows what they—are! But that remains out closest secret! You understand what I mean: here—and on the podium! […]"

Strauss celebrated his 75th and 80th birthdays with the Philharmonic (1939 and 1944, respectively), at which he also led works of his own. As a final gesture of friendship, he sent the last sketch for his tone poem *The Danube* to the orchestra in 1949, just before his death, with an apology that he was no longer able to keep his "Danube Promise."

Hans Pfitzner was made an honorary member of the Philharmonic in March 1949. The Chair of the orchestra wanted to make it possible for the aged composer to spend his final years in Vienna and received a precious gift in return: the original score of his opera *Palestrina*. Pfitzner died that May, and the autograph remains one of the prized possessions of the Philharmonic archive.

"The Vienna Philharmonic as a Propaganda Instrument"

Under this heading, Hellsberg lists the specifically "earmarked" engagements the orchestra participated in during the Nazi period: 424 concerts to benefit Nazi organizations and members of the military in occupied countries. These activities intensified as the war went on, but also kept orchestra members from having to serve on the front. The "busiest" orchestra of the "Greater German Reich" even increased its player ranks in the opera.

In this context, we should mention the New Year's Concerts, which began on December 31, 1939 under Clemens Krauss and were meant to turn the public eye from war to waltzes. According to the *Kleine Volkszeitung*, it was the task of the Vienna Philharmonic to "present the public with artistic occasions of the first rank and thus provide entertainment and edification to the home front to strengthen them in this time of heightened sorrows and needs." Now they performed this task on New Year's Morning as well.

End and New Beginning

After the proclamation of "total war" and the closing of the State Opera in 1944 (the last performance in the house was, significantly, Wagner's *Götterdämmerung*), it was the turn of orchestra members to be called up for service. The destruction of the opera house in an air raid on March 12, 1945, the seventh anniversary of the *Anschluss*, was a crisis without precedent. Fritz Sedlak, the fluent Russian-speaking concertmaster and temporary leader of the orchestra, was able to keep his orchestra as an unarmed "Volkssturmeinheit" (civilian militia unit), which was thus spared combat duty: as an "air-raid cellar collective", the musicians were used only for clearing debris and helping the wounded.

"To escape the bombings, the musicians moved to the cellar of the Burgtheater, taking their instruments, archive materials and music with them. A portion of their music was kept in concertmaster Franz Mairecker's vineyard estate," according to Merlin's summary of the dramatic last days of the war. After the burning of the Burgtheater in April 1945, these precious documents were brought back to the Musikverein, where the first concert promptly took place on April 27th. At the podium was Clemens Krauss, the only notable conductor to have stayed in Vienna, conducting the last concerts in the Third Reich—a further indicator of continuity even after the *Stunde null* (Zero hour). "And thus it came that he, who had turned his back on Austria in 1933, led the first Philharmonic concert in liberated Austria," playing "Schubert's *Unfinished* Symphony as an homage to his homeland, the Third *Leonore* overture as a fanfare for the liberation from tyranny, and the Fifth Symphony of Tchaikovsky as an obeisance to the liberators" (Blaukopf).

The decade following the war was marked by intensive work in both concert and opera (in the Theater an der Wien and the Volksoper, the two "alternative quarters" for the destroyed Opera House), but also by frequent travel in the service of a "newly awakening" Austria. Alongside the defining names Furtwängler and Knappertsbusch (just like before 1945), some of the formerly ostracized conductors such as Josef Krips, Erich Leinsdorf and Bruno Walter also took the stand.

The Denial of Responsibility

Just under 50% of the Philharmonic musicians were Nazi party members in 1945. Only five musicians, including Wilhelm Jerger, were let go immediately. According to Fritz Trümpi, it was important for the orchestra to secure "complete indemnification of the party members within their own ranks;" the majority of these "ca. 60 members" (Merlin) were protected. Not a single one of the musicians who had been driven out accepted written invitations to take back their seats in the orchestra.

The newspaper *Neues Österreich* reported that it was time "to close a painful chapter" and to "separate the present from the past," which is why the orchestra would also assume the obligation of holding concerts, "the revenues from which would flow directly into the families of the men from their ranks who became victims of National Socialism in 1938." But it soon became evident that the Philharmonic would not take this "obligation" all too seriously.

The proportion of former Nazis on the board in 1948 was striking: "a total of seven of the thirteen listed board members manifested a background that was politically implicated." Two years earlier, Leopold Wlach had uttered this statement: "We have to keep quiet for now, but soon the time will come when we can talk again." He would prove right. Helmut Wobisch was debarred from the Verein for a short time, but he returned as of April 1, 1951, and became Deputy Business Manager as early as 1952 and was promoted to Business Manager by 1953 (Trümpi). His position as trumpeter was not filled during his absence. An effective and active manager of orchestra tours, concert and recording contracts, Wobisch founded the Carinthian Summer Music Festival in 1969.

Wobisch, whom Leonard Bernstein had incidentally called his "favorite Nazi," brought "numerous NS-comrades to return to the board in June of 1952" (Trümpi) in his wake, among them the notorious Leopold Kainz. The Philharmonic maintained close contact with the expelled Wilhelm Jerger, granting him a retroactive pension without a quibble, and awarded him the Franz Schalk Medallion in 1967. Former National Socialists, among them Chairman Otto Strasser, "constituted the majority of board members until well into the sixties" (Trümpi).

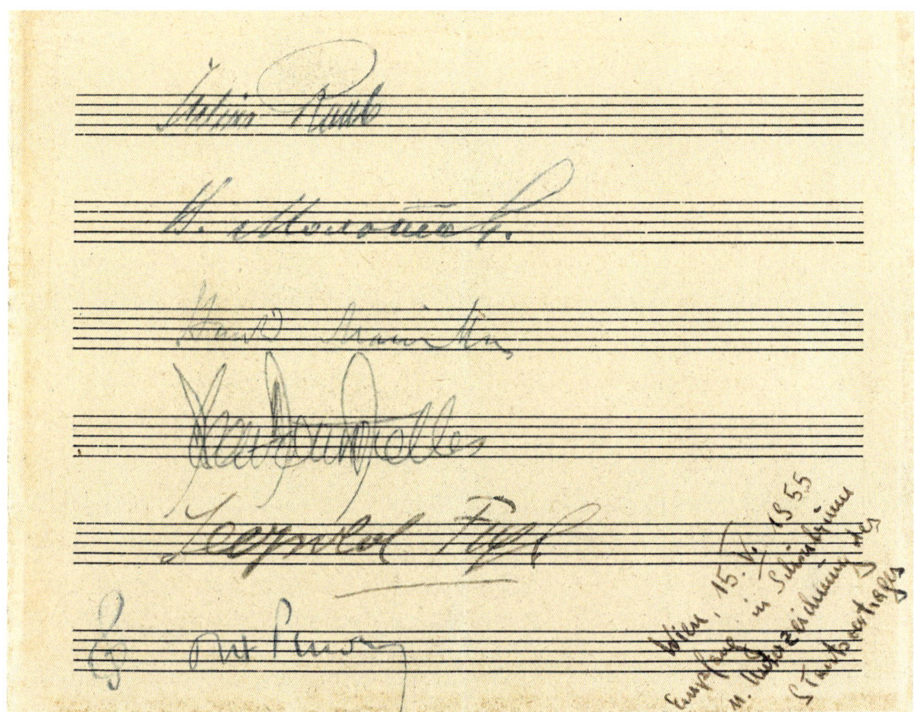

At the signing of the state treaty on May 15, 1955, violist Kurt Anders collected autographs of the foreign ministers and Federal Chancellor Julius Raab on a sheet of music.

The trenches ran right through the orchestra: the timpanist and onetime "party comrade" Hans Gärtner once made a nasty remark at a general meeting of the orchestra; Joseph Hadraba, who had only survived the orchestra's Nazi years through a special dispensation, rebuked him with these words: "Keep your mouth shut, you shameless Nazi!" The high percentage of former Nazis in the Philharmonic specifically presented problems in planning tours, but it "had absolutely no effect on anyone's thinking about de-Nazification" (Trümpi). On the contrary, the guiding principle was "that the Vienna Philharmonic travels as a whole or not at all." The forgiving Bruno Walter (who had resumed friendly relations with the orchestra again) accepted this, but not the unbending Toscanini—they had to accept that he would never return to the orchestra's desk.

However, in 1946, the "banned" Herbert von Karajan, no less, was asked to conduct a concert (which was later cancelled) for the "KZ-Verband" (concentration camp victims' organization). Of the 61 concerts that the Philharmonic presented between 1945 and 1955 "to aid charitable, diplomatic and state causes, [...] only two were for [...] organizations of 'concentration camp prisoners'", and one other was for the "Vienna State Association of once persecuted Antifascists" (Trümpi). This can be phrased positively: the orchestra's actions looked to the future (*zukunftsorientiert*), and the official demand was for nothing less than an unreserved commitment to the "new Austria." Viewed a bit more critically, the Philharmonic was used as propaganda both before and after 1945, but now for a free country.

Among the treasures stored in the State Opera's music archives are the orchestra scores for *Fidelio* dating back to the Mahler era. Concertmaster Wolfgang Schneiderhan (hired in 1937) noted in his part that Beethoven's "freedom opera" was played to mark the visit of Hermann Göring at the State Opera on March 27, 1938. Schneiderhan noted later (1946) "If only he had never come." Of course, this pious sentiment could not undo the tragedy...

Symbolic Gestures

The idea of a North American tour came up as early as 1948, but plans for it, which would also help the record business in the USA, did not become concrete until the start of the 1950s. Everyone's first choice was Furtwängler or Karajan, but their past histories made them unacceptable. After Furtwängler's death in 1954, the choice came down to the politically unproblematic conductors Carl Schuricht and André Cluytens.

It was a strategic decision to give the Nicolai Medal to the exiled colleagues Burghauser, Falk, Geringer, Salander and Wittels. Buxbaum had already received the award in England in 1947. These "symbolic gestures" were in sharp contrast to the "Philharmonic's fundamental denial of responsibility, extending even to having material support given to those who had been driven out of Austria" (Trümpi). Reparation payments in the run-up to the American tour were justified by the orchestra Chair Hermann Obermeyer in this way: "In America, we are actually largely in Jewish hands", which probably meant the US media. Legitimate petitions for pensions, such as that of Ludwig Wittels, were viewed as "mean, lowdown extortion" while Obermeyer informed the broken-down Berthold Salander: "...personally you actually had it pretty good, no bombings..."

The mother of Hans Charwat, the only Philharmonic member to die in action, was granted the lifelong full pension of an active member—an act of humanity. But, Trümpi adds, "a comparable outcome was not found for one single musician victim of National Socialism."

Trümpi's diagnosis is that the entry of former Nazis into leadership committees of the Philharmonic brought not just the "partial return of anti-Semitic prejudices," but also the conscious "disregard of any causal connection between exile and the persecution that preceded it." The strategy of "guilt rejection" regrettably coincided with the official historical image of postwar Austria and was only strengthened by the wishes of numerous surviving victims of National Socialism for reconciliation.

Confronting the Past

The process of confronting the orchestra's recent history frankly and meaningfully did not get going until the mid 1980s. The controversial figure of Federal President Kurt Waldheim, who had "faced down" his past in such an exemplarily unsatisfactory manner (i.e., by publicly suppressing it) first cast a cloud of doubt on the commonly held self-image of Austria as "Hitler's first victim." Clemens Hellsberg, leader of the Historical Archive and subsequent Board Chair, published in a program the first list of names of persecuted and murdered colleagues. He upped the ante with his 1992 volume *Demokratie der Könige*, a weighty and significant work.

Actions of high symbolic value, such as the Israel guest performance in 1998 (in which context Philharmonic Chairman Werner Resel planted trees in the "Jerusalem Peace Forest" for colleagues murdered during the National Socialist period), and the Philharmonic concert in Mauthausen concentration camp in May 2000 with Beethoven's Ninth under Simon Rattle, documented the direction in which the tradition-laden orchestra was willing to venture.

But the debate was rekindled with the publications of Harald Walser, a member of the Greens in the Federal Parliament. Walser maintained that Hellsberg had purposely left things out of his presentation of the Nazi period, in particular by suppressing the episode concerning the orchestra's Ring of Honor being restored to Baldur von Schirach and the origins of the New Year's Concerts as propaganda instruments of the Nazi period. Walser's accusations culminated in the questions: "When will the Vienna Philharmonic Orchestra finally face up to its history in the National Socialist era with no ifs ands or buts?"

Reaction came promptly. The three historians, Oliver Rathkolb, Bernadette Mayrhofer and Fritz Trümpi, who had been doing research in this area for some time, were given the official task of clarifying and making known what had happened in that era. Their findings were presented on a website in March 2013. In the same year, the families and descendants of the exiled and murdered members were invited to Vienna by the Philharmonic in cooperation with the Jewish Welcome Service. The provenance of the painting *Port-en-Bessin* by Paul Signac, which had been given to the orchestra in 1940, was researched more closely and the stolen work of art has meanwhile been restored to its owners. Silvia Kargl and Friedemann Pestel began their intensive and productive work in the Historical Archive of the Philharmonic, and they are continually coming up with new findings.

Time to Wipe the Slate Clean?

Internationally, too, signs are being put up and being written on. A several-day symposium in New York, devised and hosted by Joel Bell's "Chumir Foundation for Ethics in Leadership" in February 2014, was one such sign that attracted much attention. Within the framework of the festival "Vienna: City of Dreams" at Carnegie Hall, at which the Vienna Philharmonic played, "the history and legacy of Vienna for the last 150 years" was discussed and prominent participants—including Hellsberg and Rathkolb—pursued the question, "How the culturally sophisticated and creative society of Vienna lost its moral compass."

In his 2016 book *Nationalsozialistische Täterschaften* (*National Socialist Perpetrators*), Oliver von Wrochem writes that "the confrontation with National Socialist perpetrators and their deeds in Germany is by no means complete." The sufferings of the victims and their descendants does not allow for a "clean slate" in the sense of forgetting. The "Burden of History" mentioned in the title of this chapter knows no "expiry date" as long as human beings play a role in each other's destinies.

Concertmaster Rainer Honeck (standing) tunes his orchestra.

Sound and Tradition

What Makes the Vienna Philharmonic What It Is

If we wanted to summarize the essence of the Vienna Philharmonic in two words, the characteristics that make it unique in the whole world, they would be: sound and tradition. They are so closely connected that we can speak of a specific "sound tradition." But when we try to get to the bottom of it, we cross the frontier from perception to myth. Is the "Viennese sound" itself a myth?—In part, certainly. But myths are true, even if they contain truths that escape scientific analysis.

Such an analysis was attempted in an in-depth study by Dr. Matthias Bertsch of the Institute for Viennese Sound Style. In 2001, about 1000 people participated in an "acoustic questionnaire." The results, which varied widely from person to person depending on their musical preparation and their audience experience and which could not reduced to a common denominator, can be seen at http://drtrumpet.eu/wbny/.

"A Single Musical Instrument of Infinite Flexibility"

Let us try to get closer to the secret of the "Viennese sound" through the words of those who know the orchestra well. In the mid-sixties, when there were no women in the orchestra yet, DECCA recording chief John Culshaw praised the "instinct through which a hundred men become a single musical instrument of infinite flexibility, the sense through which these men unanimously and immediately feel the contour of a phrase, the smoothness of a crescendo. This is attained through knowing what his neighbor is doing and by performing together with him. It is a tradition that is handed down from generation to generation. This tradition has no material basis. It cannot be analyzed other than with superficial words and therefore cannot be imitated."

Christian Thielemann, speaking about the Philharmonic Ball, used a phrase that is applicable to the Vienna Philharmonic's music making: "this is what is important and what we learn again and again in Vienna: to be able to live the tradition anew." And one paragraph from Thielemann's foreword to Franz Bartolomey's family memoir explains further: "One cannot value highly enough the significance of this tradition of music-making. It is the subconscious of an orchestra that ultimately is expressed in its unique sound and specific ways of playing—and that inspires a conductor enormously. With an orchestra that—like the Viennese—plays opera and concert music at the highest level, the blind faith of the individual musicians in each other is an absolute requirement and is an essential ingredient of the "family spirit" that I so much admire in the Vienna Philharmonic."

Learning by Doing

Once upon a time, young musicians from the Court Opera Orchestra would be sat in the pit on their free evenings so they could learn, listen, and observe. Even today, the most important part of educating a Philharmonic musician takes place in the orchestra itself. "I immediately recalled Sophie"—conductor Christoph Eschenbach remembers the first orchestra appearance of the newly hired bassoonist Sophie Dartigalongue in Tokyo in 2016, "as an eminent musician who was always listening to the left and to the right: What are the others doing, how should I play together with them?" (Merz) Another example: even the more experienced solo harpist Anneleen Lenaerts orients herself to the other musicians or to the total sound desired: "Meanwhile I think about the brass, the basses, the violins at many places—and try to mold the sound of the harp accordingly."

The cellist Csaba Bornemisza recalls his early days in the State Opera orchestra: "In the first few months, you take your lead from older colleagues, following their phrasing and tone to the point that you unconsciously become part of the whole, that you feel with and breathe with the orchestra." And it was no different a generation before that, as the former solo cellist Franz Bartolomey writes: "I myself learned much from my solo colleague Robert Scheiwein's explanations in private lessons. I was willing to accept his knowledge of the playing tradition and to believe him when he said about certain passages in the big cello solo in *Frau ohne Schatten*: 'That's simply how it should be.'

The Singing Orchestra

According to Franz Bartolomey, the ability to react that one learns in the orchestra pit is one of the Philharmonic's trump cards. In the opera, which doesn't have a surplus of rehearsals but has many a run-of-the-mill repertory conductor, you have to be particularly wary!

Thanks to its daily opera duties, our orchestra attunes its sound and phrasing to the most natural instrument of all—the human voice. This ensemble experience is equally cherished by singers and orchestra players. The Viennese *Kammersänger* Kurt Rydl firmly believes: "They understand how to breathe with singers," and Bartolomey adds that the Philharmonic has acquired "its much admired sound [...], especially that of the strings, through our accompanying of the human voice."

The ever-present sound ideal of the human voice also makes the Vienna Philharmonic "sing" even when no singers are present. State Opera director Dominique Meyer is convinced: "the conductors who do well here [at the Vienna State Opera] are those that let the orchestra sing." Actual singing in the orchestra is rare but still sometimes also required of its members (for instance, in the *Bauernpolka* by Johann Strauss, Jr.), and the Philharmonic keep other vocal traditions as well, as for example in *Der Rosenkavalier*. At the beginning of Act III, when Baron Ochs asks: "...what are these cockchafers doing here?", four waiters answer him: "We're serving, your grace." In the recording studio, Erich Kleiber demanded that the musicians sing that passage. In 1954, the recording was awarded—*nota bene*, not for that reason!—the German Record Prize and the Grand Prix du disque, and the orchestra players' singing was kept on the disk for quite some time. Somewhat later in the same act, according to Ochs-singer Rydl, the musicians also sang along with the "sixteenth-note run that accompanies Annina's entrance. Thanks to the recording that was spread over the whole world, now all the orchestras from Los Angeles to Korea do it," the widely traveled bass tells us.

The Low Strings

Let us remain in the low registers. Second violinist Helmut Zehetner unrolls the secret of the sound "from underneath." In his view, the Philharmonic sound is recognizable "by the double basses. Of course from the oboe and the horns: but the sound rich with overtones comes from the way they play the basses, allowing an intensity in tone. You can build up everything else from that base." One reason for the "intensive tone" might be the way they hold the bow: while the "French bow" is held with the back of the hand up, the normal Viennese "German bow" (also known as the 'Simandl bow' after the leading player of the Mahler era) lies in the hand palm up and can effortlessly produce a floating, clear sound even on the low E string.

Like some of his colleagues and successors, Franz Simandl was a native Czech and an outstanding player of an instrument that "stood out from" all the others. (In 1913, all the double-bass players of the Philharmonic were Simandl students!) The double basses provide not just the foundation of the sound, but they also dominate optically, almost always standing at the back wall, facing the conductor.

The next higher instrument, the violoncello, most closely resembles the sound of the human voice. No episode demonstrates this more vividly than that *Lohengrin* evening under Hans Richter, during which Court Opera tenor Hermann Winkelmann had used up all his vocal reserves before the last act. Therefore, solo cellist Joseph Sulzer "sang" the Grail narrative on his instrument while Winkelmann "gestured correspondingly" on stage, as Sulzer wrote in his autobiography. Sulzer was an enigmatic character who was notoriously late for rehearsals and performances because of his many private music students. One evening he asked concertmaster Joseph Hellmesberger to let him go early because his wife was about to go into labor. Hellmesberger answered snippily: "Take your time, my dear Sulzer, your child will surely be late."

Friedrich Buxbaum's tenure as a solo cellist lasted 38 years—exceeded only by Franz Bartolomey by one year. Once a dealer asked him to try out a cello. He replied, "should I play it for buying or selling?" Another joker was Rudolf Hindemith, the composer's brother, whom Richard Strauss made a solo cellist in 1921. Hindemith managed, "during an endlessly boring

Lohengrin performance, to bowl an orange from his stand towards cello mutes he had arranged like bowling pins" (Strasser 1981).

Richard Krotschak became a solo cellist in 1934, and his student Bartolomey "inherited" the position in 1973 along with the Löwenkopf cello on which Krotschak had played Strauss' *Don Quixote* with the composer conducting. Bartolomey opined of his teacher: "he is not an analyst. For him, the most important thing is to have a big cantilena with a powerful, but never forced tone and a quiet vibrato." This is likely a prerequisite of the Viennese string sound even today, which according to Bornemisza "is created by its particular type of tone formation, bow speed and stroke." And the orchestra's "very special creative freedom" he calls "Viennese charm."

"The Viennese School"

Teacher-student relationships extending over generations are a cornerstone of Philharmonic tradition. A dry statistical comparison: in 1974, 54% of the Philharmonic violinists came from the teaching of two professors who were themselves in the Philharmonic: Franz Samohyl and Ernst Morawec. In 2011, among the teachers of 47 violinists we see Samohyl 12 times and Alfred Staar 23 times—and they had also taught three violists apiece.

The fact that Morawec was a solo violist from 1923 to 1956 and had taught just as many violinists as violists shows the permeability between the two instrument groups, for which separate training was not offered until sometime after the Second World War. (Conversely, Arnold Rosé regularly took over the viola solos in the opera and concerts.) Morawec was a strict teacher from whom the following *bon mot* has come down: "A series of wrong notes is still not a chromatic scale!"

For Franz Samohyl, who among others was the teacher of concertmasters Rainer Küchl and Werner Hink, the ideal education was "a solo training, through which the future musician would acquire the ability to solve technical problems in the orchestra as well" (Blaukopf). Samohyl was so absorbed in his pedagogical activities that he gave up his membership in the Verein of the Vienna Philharmonic in order to concentrate on opera and theory. Alfred Staar, whose instruction produced concertmaster Rainer

Honeck among others, wanted to convey to his students “how beautiful it is to play in the orchestra.”

Of course, the Viennese violin tradition extends considerably further back than just two or three generations. A direct line exists from Morawec to Rosé back to Joseph Hellmesberger, Senior, as well as another branch leading from Walter Barylli and Willi Boskovsky via the concertmasters Mairecker, Stwertka and Grün back to Joseph Böhm, who is considered the ‘father’ of the Viennese violin school. Böhm was born in Budapest in 1795 and learned his art from a Frenchman (Pierre Rode), who in turn was the student of an Italian (Giovanni Battista Viotti). The Czech violinist Otakar Ševčík (graduate of the Prague Conservatory, as was the double-bass player Simandl and the clarinetist Barolomey) also left his mark on the Viennese style. Do these international intermixtures argue against a “Viennese” school? We will return to this question at the end of the chapter.

What a Concertmaster/Concertmistress does

The man (or, since 2008 in the Philharmonic, the woman) in this conspicuous position is the section leader for the first violins, responsible for the violin solos and for direct communication with the conductor. And particularly with the Philharmonic, the concert master has the job of embodying and continuing the specific performing tradition of the orchestra. “When Rainer Honeck speaks, he is always talking about style,” recalls Dominique Meyer about many an orchestra audition in the State Opera.

This direction-setting figure is also required to respond to exceptional situations. Strasser (1981) reports: “I have had situations when one of the violin soloists’ strings broke during a concert, as happened with Ginette Neveu and Wolfgang Schneiderhan. Each time Concertmaster Walter Barylli gave them his own violin.” Sometimes the concertmaster intervenes in grander style when the conductor loses his place. This happened in May of 1875 when Richard Wagner was conducting *Siegfried’s Funeral March*. The brass and the strings were starting to drift apart, “at which point [Joseph] Hellmesberger [Senior] got up from his chair and, by energetically beating time and tempo, restored order.”

Otherwise it was and remains uncommon for the concertmaster to get up from his chair during solos (just as uncommon as coming onstage separately after the orchestra has been seated). Concertmaster Jakob Grün (hired in 1868) had to deal with Joseph Hellmesberger junior's sharp tongue after he asked him whether he should play the violin solo in Beethoven's *Missa solemnis* sitting or standing. The latter answered: "Just stay in your chair and let the solo stand." Hellmesberger's statement "Grün (green) is good for the eyes but bad for the ears," is not exactly evidence of mutual collegiality.

Early in the 1960s, 21-year-old Günter Pichler, coming from the Vienna Symphony Orchestra, was on temporary trial as concertmaster and was determined to prove himself. Merlin gives us this anecdote: "Once, Karl Böhm supposedly turned to [Concertmaster Willi] Boskovsky during rehearsal and asked: 'Why is the guy playing so loud?', whereupon Boskovsky answered with a knowing smile: 'He's playing for the job!'" Günter Pichler did not become concertmaster of the Philharmonic but the leader of the Alban Berg Quartet, which he founded in 1970. Let us now turn to chamber music.

Chamber Music

When Erich Kleiber returned to the podium of the Vienna Philharmonic after the Second World War, his first question was how many chamber music groups there were in the orchestra. If accompanying voices is *one* important element in finding the right sound, since it is reacting to "others" that trains one how to lead and follow, then chamber music, the listening *to one another*, is a second element. Hans Swarowsky, who taught a generation of top conductors, thought: "Quartet culture is the backbone of all good string sound! Just as a wind octet should be created from the orchestra with the most finely detailed training in chamber playing. String quartet and wind ensemble should complement each other in mixed compositions."

Most members of the Philharmonic first violin section devote themselves to chamber music, and these ensembles often bore and bear the names of sitting concertmasters. This tradition started with Joseph Hellmesberger, Senior, who premiered works of Beethoven, Schubert, Brahms and

Bruckner. His sons Joseph and Ferdinand also joined the quartet, which existed until 1901.

Over the decades from 1883 until 1938, when it was forcibly disbanded, a total of ten Philharmonic members played in the Rosé Quartet. The list of world premieres the quartet gave extends from Brahms to Schönberg (*Verklärte Nacht* and the 1st and 2nd string quartets) and on to Franz Schmidt and Hans Pfitzner. After the First World War, the Rosé Quartet played guest concerts in Scandinavia—a welcome source of income at a time of economic crisis. At the final concert in a small town in Sweden, the mayor ended his speech thanking them with these words: "We only hope that the economic situation in Austria gets better soon and that Herr Rosé will be able to enlarge his four-man-orchestra accordingly!"

After the turn of the century, other quartets were led by concertmasters Jakob Grün, Karl Prill, Julius Stwertka and Wolfgang Schneiderhan (with Otto Strasser, Ernst Morawec and Richard Krotschak). After Schneiderhan resigned (1949), the Boskovsky, Barylli and Weller Quartets followed. The Weller Quartet's second violinist Alfred Staar coached the Küchl Quartet, founded in 1973, and plays a cycle in the Vienna Musikverein to this day. Volkhard Steude, with the ensemble bearing his name, not only continues Rosé's tradition of a concertmaster quartet, but for a long while he also played on a Stradivarius belonging to Arnold Rosé, which was placed at his disposal by the Österreichische Nationalbank. And concertmistress Albena Danailova made music together with Raimund Lissy, the second violin section leader, and the violist Michael Strasser in the "Ensemble Wien."

Starting with the 2010 season, the State Opera has provided various different Philharmonic chamber music ensembles with the opportunity of concertizing in the Gustav Mahler Hall. A high point of the series came in April 2017 when the Japanese violinist Midori played Brahms and Schubert with Philharmonic colleagues (among others the series' organizer, first violinist and, as of fall 2017, new Orchestra Chair Daniel Froschauer). Notable as well are the "PhilBass Quartet," the crossover ensembles "The Philharmonics" and "Philharmonic Five," founded by second violinist Tibor Kovác, the "K + K Plattform" of first violinist Kirill Kobantschenko and many others.

The "Viennese Instruments"

All the instrument groups have their tradition of sound that is gently phrased, flowing, and not too much vibrato: a sound that even at *fortissimo* is never harsh. With the strings, clarinets, and bassoons, there are schools that go back a long way that guarantee the "correct" way to play them. Horn and oboe are exceptions even in terms of structure, a type used only in Vienna that has had a lasting effect on the characteristic sound of the orchestra.

The Viennese horn in F is an original instrument from Beethoven's era. A dyed-in-the-wool Viennese opera-goer would not want to hear Leonore's big aria in *Fidelio* with any other accompaniment! The double horn, which since the turn of the century has established itself everywhere else, may be less risky to play and not as apt to have breaks in tone ("hiccups"), but the warmth and fullness of sound of the Viennese horn inspired Brahms, Bruckner and Mahler and is indispensable for romantic music.

If we compare two critics separated by a century, we can recognize the value of tradition. The *Wiener Fremdenblatt* noted in December 1869 on a performance of the *Eroica*, "Even good fortune was allied with this performance, for the notorious horn passage in the trio of the scherzo movement, which no angel or devil has in his power, were beautiful and smooth." And in the *New York Times* in September 1967: "The flowing, gentle sound of the Philharmonic's strings has become a trademark of the group, but one wonders where the orchestra finds so many excellent hornists."

Legendary hornists such as Josef Schantl and Karl Stiegler (whose brothers Adolf and Hans were Philharmonic trumpeters) have continued the tradition of teaching as well as playing into the twentieth century. When Stiegler died in 1932 at only 57, Bruno Walter sent a moving letter to the Philharmonic on this "ideal" hornist: "He had Romantic nobility of tone and expression and the powerful blast of the hunting instrument, and with all that the virtuosity and certainty of the modern brass player." This tradition lives and is well networked in with that of the other instrument groups, as hornist Thomas Jöbstl confirms: "The ability to vary the sound from very soft and supple all the way to very powerful and blaring makes the Viennese horn a unique link between woodwinds and brass." (Lammerhuber)

Josef Reif in the Basilica San Paolo fuori le Mura in Rome

The Viennese oboe is actually a product of Saxony. The solo oboist Richard Baumgärtel (hired in 1880), who came from Dresden, established the instrument permanently in the orchestra and gave instruction on it to musicians such as Alexander Wunderer, Hans Kamesch and Armin Tyroler. Other orchestras employ the French oboe, which is played with an intense vibrato as opposed to the Viennese oboe. The French sound is described as more "nasal" (if not "bleating" or "plaintive"). After a postwar guest appearance of the orchestra in England, the newspapers complained about the missing oboe vibrato, to which Strasser responded coolly, “Let them play their funeral march *lamentoso*; for our part, as Furtwängler once said, we prefer our grief without tears.”

The obligation to play other woodwind instruments (oboe d’amore, English horn and heckelphone) when necessary tempted the oboist Hans Hanak to play a joke: He “brought a disciplinary hearing upon himself because he played the second oboe part of a Brahms symphony on the English horn” (Merlin). One of today’s oboe soloists, Martin Gabriel, complains “that unfortunately, there has never been a proper oboe school in Vienna, as there is for clarinetists, flutists, or bassoonists, for example—and that is only compared with the other woodwinds; yet each of the Vienna oboists tries in his own personal way to live up to the Vienna musical tradition” (Lammerhuber).

Woodwinds

Turning now to the last mentioned instruments: the flute is counted as a woodwind, although the orchestra instrument has long been made of gold, silver, stainless steel, or other metals. The Viennese flute has not taken hold here (as opposed to the horn and the oboe), but instead a flute originally designed in the 1830s by the German instrument maker Theobald Böhm, for whom it is named. A Dutch flutist, Ary van Leeuwen, who was hired by Mahler, brought the stronger-sounding Böhm flute with him into the orchestra. His compatriot Jacques van Lier followed four years later with the same instrument. A decisive difference for the Viennese sound even today, however, is that it is played with little or no vibrato.

The granddaddy of the Viennese clarinet school was Franz Bartolomey (whose role as founder of a Philharmonic dynasty will be touched on later). On the occasion of the Salzburg Mozart Festival of 1901, the *New York Tribune* wrote about Bartolomey’s artistry: “Whoever has not heard him play his instrument does not know how sweet a clarinet can sound!” He taught at the conservatory from 1898 until 1920 and was indirectly responsible for almost all the clarinetists who came after: the line reaches all the way to Daniel Ottensamer, whose father Ernst was also a solo clarinetist.

The Viennese Sound—
this time luxuriating in
the cloister of San Paolo

Daniel Ottensamer (in Lammerhuber) mentions the special fabrication of the mouthpieces and their respective reeds (which all reed instrumentalists must make for themselves) along with "the particular character of the Viennese sound" in the clarinets, which "blends in well with the orchestra and always sounds harmonic and pleasant in the *tutti* passages. It is possible, however, for the clarinet to stand out with its special lustrous sound in solo passages."

The old Viennese bassoon has likewise not been retained; it was exchanged in the late 19th century for instruments made in Dresden by the Heckel firm. With this instrument, too, there is a dynasty of players and teachers on hand: the brothers Karl and Camillo Öhlberger and Karl's son Reinhard. The outstanding pedagogue Karl Öhlberger declared that "the distinctive mark of the Viennese school is: we have no vibrato." These days it is used sparingly depending on the repertory: the recently arrived bassoonist Sophie Dartigalongue put it aptly: a "very fine, warm sound with somewhat less vibrato."

Once again, we notice that the various groups of instruments even fit themselves to each other. Michael Werba (pupil of Karl Öhlberger and teacher of Benedikt Dinkhauser): "Through the influence of the Viennese string sound as well as the special intonation of the Viennese horn and the Viennese oboe, even the bassoon eventually developed a very particular Viennese way of playing. It is distinguished by a special richness of overtones and allows an extremely wide range in dynamics."

Hornist Karl Stiegler and oboist Alexander Wunderer comparing their instruments.

Woodwinds at work: first row (from left): Wolfgang Breinschmid, Walter Auer, Clemens Horak, Herbert Maderthaner; back row (from left): Gregor Hinterreiter, Ernst Ottensamer, Štěpán Turnovský, Wolfgang Koblitz

Brass Instruments

Many woodwind players rely on collaboration with the Japanese instrument manufacturer Yamaha. This is also true of the brass players, for whom there are now excellent workshops in Austria, such as the Jungwirth firm.

The most prominent member of the brass family is the trumpet. The Philharmonic exclusively uses Viennese three-valve trumpets, which have a somewhat larger bore and mouthpiece, which, analogously to the horn, are somewhat more demanding to play, but have a nobler and gentler sound. Here, the decisive difference is not how it is constructed but the special idea of the sound being attuned to the other instrument groups: "You can justifiably speak of a special Viennese trumpet sound that was passed on through the decades and further developed," says solo trumpeter Hans Peter Schuh (Lammerhuber).

New instruments—traditional sound ideal: this is also the case with the trombones. The old style valve trombone (which Brahms still wrote for in

A Philharmonic trombonist on the balcony of the Shanghai Symphony Hall

his Second Symphony) was used until the 1880s, when it gave way to the more modern slide trombone. But the style of play, in the best Viennese tradition, is softer, rounder and more *cantabile*. Strasser in 1981 tells of a musician—without naming him—who took a certain liberty in the 3rd act of *Rosenkavalier* at Baron Ochs' exit: "in earlier days a particular trombonist used to insert a counter-voice right into the middle of the ¾ time hullabaloo—the tune of "Oh, du lieber Augustin" [Austrian folk tune], which strangely enough no conductors objected to."

The tuba was incorporated in the orchestra relatively late. Franz Fretzer was engaged as the player of the "Bombardon" in the mid-1850s, but the big jobs for the instruments didn't appear until Wagner's operas. As with the trombone, there was no separate instruction for the tuba. The double bass teacher supplied this at the conservatory. And for this instrument, too, there is a special Viennese form, about which the Philharmonist Josef Hummel said in the 1980s: "The Viennese tuba will die with me." But the lighter, brighter sounding instrument is still used in certain cases today.

Harp and Percussion

One outstanding master of the orchestra's only plucked instrument was Antonio Zamara, a Philharmonic musician and important teacher from 1842 to 1892, whose school produced Franz Jelinek as well. (*His* father, Franz Senior, was a solo violist who led a salon orchestra on the side and presented the orchestra with a total of three sons.) Jelinek once fell asleep in rehearsal during a long pause in the music. When his solo was supposed to come, there was…nothing. Before the concert on the next day, a colleague asked him cattily: "So, Franz, will you play your solo again today?" to which the harpist purred: "No, today I'm sleeping at home."

The solo harpist Harald Kautzky revealed his secret for a more supple sound: "wearing down the thumbtips," and he insisted that he could make better weather predictions than any meteorologist based on the variations in pitch of his instrument. Ultimately the harpist position cleared the way for women to enter the orchestra—but more of that later.

The percussion section is the most extensive group, comprising countless individual instruments ranging from the familiar kettledrum

to the marimba, all the way to the lotus flute (bird whistle). In earlier centuries, the percussion section was considered a "pasture" to which older orchestra members would be consigned. Today it is a highly specialized troop that understands how to deal with the challenges of modern music. Percussion instruments are in constant evolution, but there are also Viennese specialities like the little brass drum. The triangle and the glockenspiel created a very gentle, bright sound "thanks to a special metal alloy," according to the Philharmonic percussionist Benjamin Schmidinger, "while the cymbals, modeled on old Turkish instruments, possess a heavier and darker sound that mixes very well with the sound of the brass of our orchestra." (Lammerhuber)

The Viennese pedal kettledrum differs fundamentally from that of other orchestras: the drumhead stretched over it is made exclusively of goatskin

The famous etching by Ferdinand Schmutzer: to the left of the picture, the timpanist Hans Schnellar, Felix Weingartner conducting (1923)

Richard Strauss signed a manuscript of the last page of his *Sinfonia domestica* dedicated to "my dear Vienna Philharmonic in admiration and gratitude for many hours of sublime artistic enjoyment, most devotedly yours" (1932).

(elsewhere artificial materials or calfskin is used) and the sticks used to play them have heads of cork. They have a mechanism used to change the tuning that "doesn't move the drumhead up or down, but rather moves the kettle through a lever action so it can move more freely." (Lammerhuber) This system was developed by the Philharmonic timpanist Hans Schnellar. He was so highly esteemed by Mahler that he tried to take him back to the New York Philharmonic. Because this did not work out, Mahler just ordered "Schnellar-timpani" for his new orchestra. Schnellar's system is still being further developed by his students and successors to the present day.

Merlin writes that Schnellar was "an extremely difficult personality." He was once reported "for cleaning his timpani with gasoline, which was an offense against all the safety regulations and aroused the attention of the fire department." Schnellar got in the habit of leaving *Aida* performances before the end until conductor Hugo Reichenberger noticed that "the final G-flat chord was missing its foundation, and from then on the sinner had no choice but to wait until the death of the two lovers on stage." Schnellar made a name for himself not just through breaking the regulations, but also a compositional intervention in Strauss' *Sinfonia domestica*: he "expanded his part by transposing the motif almost completely to his own instrument using seven notes and four timpani, which increased the effect enormously. Strauss, who may first have heard this 'version' on the South American tour in 1923, approved of the change." (Merlin)

One more percussionist personality must be mentioned: Franz Broschek was the semi-official prankster of the Philharmonic's New Year's Concerts for years. Witeschnik recalls the origins of the pranks, which date from a concert played by the orchestra under Karl Böhm on tour in Böhm's home town of Graz in the 1950s. At a restaurant party, the innkeeper handed out false beards and mustaches to his musical guests. "At the next New Year's concert, the percussionist Franz Broschek found his fake twirled moustache in his briefcase and, still in a New Year's Eve mood, put it on for the fast polka number *Éljen a Magyar* (Johann Strauss, Junior). It was a resounding comic success with the audience! And so Broschek became the "must-have joker" at the annual waltz concerts. "For the *Radetzky* March he strutted across the podium in regimental *Deutschmeister* garb, and in the *Krapfenwaldl* polka he made the cuckoo so love-crazed that he called in off-key thirds, and after the polka *The Hunt* he would drag a huge codfish or a plucked chicken onstage, in the *Champagne Polka* corks would pop and he would pour concertmaster/conductor/violinist Willi Boskovsky an overflowing glass."

Composing Philharmonists

Let us take a few composing gentlemen from the first 100 years of the Philharmonic. Flutist Franz Doppler, a member of the Court Opera Orchestra from 1858, was a professor at the conservatory, ballet conductor and composer of ballet music such as *Melusine* and once beloved operettas such as *Ilka und die Husarenwerbung* (*Ilsa, or: the Hussar Recruitment*).

On his travels he met Franz Liszt, whose *Hungarian Rhapsodies* he edited. The Symphony in C minor of orchestra director Moritz Kässmayer was premiered in March 1863 at the same subscription concert in which Brahms' Second Serenade in A was christened. The Vienna-born Ludwig Alois (Louis) Minkus was the orchestra's first violinist for a short time (1852) before he switched to composing ballet music (for example *The Bayadere* and *Don Quixote.*) Josef Bayer stayed at the second violin desk for 28 years, and his ballet *Die Puppenfee* (*The Doll Fairy*) also became world famous.

The works of Joseph Hellmesberger, Junior, representing the third generation of his family to hold the position of concertmaster, were repeatedly selected for the New Year's Concerts. Programs included: his fast polka *Leichtfüßig* (*Light-footed*) in 1997, his *Valse Espagnole* in 2009, the *Gypsy Dance* from his operetta *Die Perle von Iberien* in 2011, his *Danse diabolique* in 2012, the polka mazur *Unter vier Augen* (*Tête-à-tête*) in 2013, and *Vielliebchen, polka française* in 2014. In 2016, it was Joseph Hellmesberger, Senior's, turn, with *Ballszene*, the transcription of a violin sonata by Josef Mayseder.

The hornists Josef Schantl, Karl Stiegler and Wilhelm Kleinecke, the oboist Alexander Wunderer and the second violinist Hermann Grädener were also among the orchestra's composers, as well as first violinist Josef Klein. Both ballet music (*Faun und Nymphe*) and light music came from Klein's pen, among other things an *Elektra* Waltz, a popularization of the opera by Richard Strauss in the best tradition of Johann Strauss. The violinist Hugo Riesenfeld left the Vienna orchestra in 1907 and headed for New York. After engagements with Oscar Hammersteins I.'s Manhattan Opera Company and in a Broadway theater, he became the musical head of United Artists and the creator of over 100 film scores.

Cellist Franz Schmidt first came to the Philharmonic in 1896. He was in constant conflict with the concertmaster and director Arnold Rosé, who advised his boss Mahler not to promote Schmidt to solo cello. The situation escalated when Schmidt was ordered to jump in at the last minute as a soloist in *Walküre*, which he flatly refused to do. "Neither the official communication from the orchestra's messenger nor Rosé's brutal threats could move me to trade my seat for the soloist position […] Mahler understood the situation with one glance, but kept a poker-face." The performance went on with no cello soloist at all, "but they didn't fire me."

Franz Schmidt: "To the Vienna Philharmonic in memory of their colleague"

Overall, it seems that Schmidt performed his duties in the orchestra according to regulations but used the time for his own creative activities. After a particularly boring performance of *Pagliacci*, he confided to the oboist Wunderer that during the performance he had thought of a theme: this was to become the main theme of the dungeon scene of *Notre Dame*. The Victor Hugo-inspired work was premiered in 1914 at the Vienna Court Opera after it had already been rejected by Gustav Mahler and Felix Weingartner. Schmidt had left the orchestra in 1911 to devote himself completely to his composing and teaching work. His skills as a pianist were also known to the virtuoso Leopold Godowsky, who asserted: "There are actually only two people who can really play the piano…the other is Franz Schmidt."

Composers after 1945

We shall limit ourselves to the gentlemen whose works were honored with a Philharmonic premiere. In 1952, Knappertsbusch conducted the *Dance Suite* by oboist Hans Hadamowsky; and Karajan conducted the *Rhapsodic Sketches* of first violinist Fritz Leitermeyer in 1963.

Clarinetist Alfred Prinz, who was hired at only fifteen years of age by the State Opera orchestra in 1945, was present for the premiere of his *Music for Orchestra*, conducted by Horst Stein. The violist Paul Walter Fürst composed numerous works for his instrument. His opus 54, titled *Omedeto*, is for twelve violas, and he also arranged the Strauss works *Kaiserwalzer* and *Unter Donner und Blitz* (*Thunder and Lightning*) for a dozen violas.

To name just one work of the recently retired first violinist, teacher and internationally successful composer René Staar: his orchestral work *Time Recycling* was given its world premiere at the Musikverein under Semyon Bychkov; Gustavo Dudamel conducted it at the Salzurg Festival the same year, and it accompanied the Philharmonic on its USA tour with Franz Welser-Möst in 2017.

Light Music and other Arts

In 1981, Otto Strasser arrogantly called popular musicians "renegades" or "heretics" and suspected that Benny Goodman "recuperated from jazz with Mozart's clarinet concerto." But in truth, the orchestra was welcoming all along to performers of folk and popular music. In 1886, Eduard Strauss estimated the number of Philharmonic musicians who had a background in the Strauss orchestra at no fewer than 27!

The orchestra performed a carnival concert on February 15, 1952, in the Great Hall of the Musikverein with the title: *Die Wiener Philharmoniker Einmal Anders* (*The Vienna Philharmonic...with a Difference*). Rudolf Streng (later a solo violist), violinists Fritz Leitermeyer and Karl Rosner, saxophonist Rudy Jettel (as a Philharmonic clarinetist he went by "Rudolf"!), and the trombonist Josef Hadraba were not only on stage, but their works were played as well. The Hans Faltl Quartet was also there and played a *Quodlibet* by its eponymous composer. It should be noted that they were almost all pieces from the "light muse."

On the last evening of the Japan tour under Herbert von Karajan in 1959, there was a reception at the Austrian Embassy, at which Faltl and his *Schrammel*-players performed waltzes. A relaxed maestro sat down at the piano and played along. Faltl reminded him: "Just be sure to stay in G major, Herr von Karajan, and nothing can happen!"

The first violinist Karl Machek played with a popular folk music quartet, whose founder was the Philharmonic contrabassist Karl Schreinzer; these days the violinists Johannes Tomböck and Dominik Hellsberg are members of the "Philharmonia Schrammeln." Rudolf Jettel came to the Philharmonic from the world of popular music; the Bartolomey student Karl (or Charley when playing saxophone) Gaudriot led a successful double life, as did the trombonist Rudolf Josel, founder of the Josel Trio and frequent jazz partner of Friedrich Gulda among others. Georg Breinschmid, brother of flutist Wolfgang Breinschmid, was part of the State Opera orchestra from 1996 to 1998 before it pulled him into another repertoire—today he is the most respected jazz bass player in Austria.

But there were also other side careers, which should at least receive brief mention here. Violist Rudolf Zöllner became mayor of Baden bei Wien, and his instrumental colleague Gottfried Martin, also Business Manager of the State Opera orchestra, was a professional painter on the side, as was Hans Novak, the caricaturist, before him. The cellist Karl Udel founded a popular singing quartet that was so highly esteemed that the local authorities in Vienna erected a cenotaph in his honor. The double bass group has produced two painters, Adolf Dürrer and Franz Holub, about whom one colleague joked: "The one paints genuine Holubs, the other only fake Dür(r)ers."

Dynastic Matters

If we wanted to determine which Philharmonic descendants have come to rank and influence in Austria, that would probably require an entire book on its own. So only two examples: Franz Patay, current Business Manager of the United Stages of Vienna, is the son of the violist Georg Patay. And Austria's most beloved comedian of the middle generation, Michael Niavarani, is the grandson of Gustav Swoboda. To quote Niavarani: "My grandfather was first violinist at the Philharmonic—they didn't have one before that!?" This sense of humor must have been present with his

The Hellmesberger brothers Georg, Junior, and Joseph, Senior

grandfather, for when Swoboda retired, he sighed happily, “At last I can practice in peace!”

Even confining ourselves to family relationships within the orchestra, a few “highlights” will have to suffice. The first and up to now probably most important “dynasty” was that of the Hellmesbergers, who were active in the orchestra for over 80 years and had four Philharmonists in three generations. The orchestra director Georg I. had participated in the world premiere of the Beethoven’s Ninth in 1824. His son, Joseph I., was the far better violinist according to Otto Nicolai, a concertmaster as well, a founder of a string quartet, conductor of the association concerts of the Gesellschaft der Musikfreunde and the director of their conservatory. There is a charming anecdote linked to his leadership in the Court Chapel Orchestra (*Hofmusikkapelle*). The famous Court Opera tenor Gustav

Walter would regularly send his brother to substitute for him at the Sunday church concerts. When Walter himself came back one day, Hellmesberger greeted him with: "Good Morning, Herr Kammersänger, I do hope that your brother is not ill!"

Joseph I. had two "Philharmonic sons" (Georg Junior lived in Hannover and died young), namely Ferdinand, who was a cellist for 14 years and then a professor at the conservatory, where he taught (among others) Franz Schmidt and Friedrich Buxbaum; and Joseph Junior, concertmaster in the third generation, opera conductor, subscription series conductor as well as a prolific composer, as we have mentioned above. Merlin sums up Hellmersberger's playing style as the essence of Viennese musicianship when he says, "the quality of his style is based less on technical precision and virtuosity than on refinement and sensitivity."

Franz I., Franz II., and Franz III. Bartolomey

Philharmonists for 120 years

In 1892, the Czech clarinetist František Bartolomej won the competitive audition (*Concurrenzspiel*) for the position of solo clarinetist. But the director of the National Theater in Prague did not want to let him go and warned his Viennese colleagues in this touching fashion: "...Bartolomej can't speak nothing German!"

We have already mentioned Franz I. Bartolomey's fabulous playing and the enduring effect of his teaching, so let us now identify his Philharmonic progeny: the violinist Franz II., pupil of the concertmaster Mairecker, joined the orchestra in 1938—his invitation "for the final round" of auditions already bore the salutation "Heil Hitler!". Franz II., who was a very active Vice Chairman and after his retirement became Intendant of the Vienna

Daniel, Ernst and Andreas Ottensamer

Symphony Orchestra, had two sons: Ernst, a student of Samohyl, who was in the second violin section from 1966 until 1992 and died at the age of only 53 in 1996. Franz III., trained by Philharmonic solo cellist Ewald Winkler, Richard Krotschak and Emanuel Brabec, was a member of the orchestra from 1967 until 2012 and a solo cellist for 39 of those years. His son Matthias is a cellist as well, not with the Philharmonic, but rather has found a career among other things with the Concentus Musicus of Nikolaus Harnoncourt and in the crossover duo team BartolomeyBittmann.

Alois Schmidl joined the orchestra in the same year as Franz I. Bartolomey, whose family germanized its name somewhat more thoroughly (the original name was Kowalsky). His family was in the orchestra almost as long as the Bartolomeys, but with hiatuses. Alois was a member from 1892 to 1914, his son Viktor from 1921 to 1936, his grandson Peter from 1965 to 2010. Peter Schmidl was an influential figure: first solo clarinetist, Business Manager of the Philharmonic (2001 to 2005), and finally the doyen of the Vienna State Opera (from 2006). A large number of his students at the Musikuniversität Wien found their way to the Philharmonic, including Johann Hindler, Norbert Täubl, Andreas Wieser, Ernst, who unexpectedly passed away in 2017, and his son Daniel Ottensamer.

Touching now on the Tomböck family: Wolfgang Senior was succeeded by son Wolfgang Junior as solo hornist in 1983, and grandson Johannes Tomböck is a first violin. The first in the "female line of succession" of the Philharmonic is second violinist Patricia Hood-Koll, daughter of the solo violist Heinrich Koll.

The Standard Keeps Improving

The educational institution that was founded in 1817 and has taken on various names through the years, such as Conservatory, Academy of Music and the Performing Arts, and Musikhochschule, is known today as the Vienna University for Music and the Performing Arts. In 1909, the year it was nationalized, 27 Philharmonic members were on the faculty (including celebrities such as the concertmasters Rosé, Prill and Stwertka, the cellist Buxbaum, the double bassist Simandl, the oboist Baumgärtel, the harpist Zamara and the timpanist Schnellar). Today, the number of teachers from

Vienna's top orchestra is about a dozen. At Vienna's private University for Music and Art (MUK: Musik und Kunst), the other university level teaching institution in the Austrian capital, there are currently five Philharmonic players on the faculty.

Back in the mid-1980s, Wolfgang Herzer, a solo cellist from 1973 till 2005, asserted that "the standard for a degree exam a quarter century ago [so early 1960s: tr.] was no higher than that of a normal evening class at the Musikhochschule." And the standard continues to go up…

Bottom Line: is there a Viennese Sound?

A Philharmonist cannot even reliably recognize his own orchestra: first violinist Andreas Großbauer took a test in which five different versions of the *Fledermaus* overture were played for him. It was the Vienna Philharmonic each time, but under five different conductors! The influence of the musical director must not be underestimated and cannot be overestimated…

Otto Strasser worried in 1981 that "following a general trend towards 'norm'-alization, one day the Vienna Philharmonic could develop into an orchestra that is stylistically international and will forget its musical 'Viennessity.'" Solo violist Heinrich Koll sees the "language problem" in a more nuanced fashion: "We speak a dialect. When we 'homogenize' it too much, it will die." On the other hand, Matthias Schorn, a solo clarinetist from the Salzburger Land, has another opinion, namely, that one can appropriate a "musical dialect:" "the unmistakability of the Philharmonic sound, this musicianship having nothing to do with nationality—this is what we have to preserve." (Merz)

Christian Thielemann referred to an older colleague, in whose tradition he definitely can see himself: "I should especially like to emphasize their extraordinary flexibility—every time the sound is unique, a 'natural product' that absolutely cannot be attained 'via technical *dressage*,' created by a 'troop of top rank virtuosi,' to quote the words of Wilhelm Furtwängler."

This same Furtwängler, the head conductor of the Wiener Tonkünstler Orchestra (predecessor of today's Vienna Symphony) in the early 1920s, visited the Philharmonic concerts and was impressed by the "peculiarly lustrous sound of the strings." Someone assured him that this came from the instruments, which were made in the Viennese workshop of Gabriel Lembröck (of which there are still a few in use today). When the young conductor tried outfitting his orchestra with these wonderful instruments, it turned out that the sound was "duller and more lackluster than usual." "It is not simply the instruments that make the music, […] nor the 'school,' nor is it ability—it's the people and the personal attitude towards life behind their artistic accomplishment that is the real agent." We are reminded of the composer's words in the prelude to *Ariadne auf Naxos*: "When I say: the violins, I mean the players!"

Today there are more and more women among these players, who bring a fresh approach to "classical" music, like Patricia Hood-Koll: "This organized sloppiness, that's our strong point: Get those emotions out there and touch people." (Merz)

At a guest performance of the Meininger Hofkapelle in 1904, the Philharmonic violinist Stefan Wahl compared that orchestra with his own. The Meiningen musicians "did not so much beat us as astound us, mainly through the precision and exactness of their ensemble play. […] But as far as warmth and energy went, we pretty much won hands down." So while the German orchestra employed an almost military discipline, the more multiculturally oriented Austrians were the experts for feeling and expression—a view that still exists today. Wahl summed up: "To a certain extent, we play the mediating role of the temperate zone that balances out the opposites of North and South."

This explanation reminds us of another, even older text from the pen of Franz Grillparzer. His hymn of praise to Austria in the drama *King Ottokar's Rise and Fall* (1825) already includes the geographical and national antagonisms that Austria is seen as having to overcome: "O good country, O fatherland! Between Italy the baby and Germany the man you lie, a red cheeked boy, and make that good, that others bring to ruin."

Here we are dealing not with a musical, but an Austrian myth. What is Austrian in general and Viennese in particular is the mixture of German, Slavic, Hungarian, Jewish and Mediterranean influences. So it was in the multi-ethnic state, whose 'child' the Philharmonic is, and so it is with the composition and special sound of the orchestra even today. Just as Vienna was always a melting pot, musicians then and now from every geographic and stylistic direction work together here, and among them the "German" influence was never dominant. But let us also not forget the favorite Philharmonic composers, the three capital B's (Beethoven, Brahms, Bruckner) as well as Mozart, and none of them actually came from Vienna.

The last word of this chapter belongs to a Frenchman, Dominique Meyer, who as a cultural manager has attained great familiarity with the Vienna Philharmonic: "We will never know all the secrets of this sound. Thank God."

Congratulatory letter from the chorus of the Court Opera on the 50th anniversary of the Philharmonic Subscription Concerts (1910)

"How Do I Get to the Philharmonic?"

And: How the Philharmonic Got to Where It Is

The joke is all too familiar. A traveler arrives at the West train station and asks the taxi driver the above question. The driver carefully answers: "practice, practice, practice!"

The First Rules of Order

But let us also ask how the institution developed, how the Philharmonic got to where it is. Even Otto Nicolai had twice presented statutes for signing, but the first actual rules of order of the "Philharmonic Concert Undertaking" are from the year 1862. It made clear that no concert entrepreneur, but the free association of professional artists would make the decisions. It was specified that at least once a year, a general meeting ("General-Versammlung") would take place that would decide on the choice of conductor and the composition of the twelve-member "Comite", that is, the administrative body (which the conductor headed until 1898). And an allocation key for dividing up the total received income was also agreed upon, by which the conductor would receive three shares, the concertmaster two shares and all other members one share. In case of sickness—and this is a significant social advance—the member would still be paid his full allotment. Finally, the music archive was set up and a democratic process begun by which the inclusion of new pieces would be decided in the framework of the so-called "Novitätenproben" (new work tryouts).

Blaukopf summarizes: "the Philharmonic constitution, which back in 1862 envisaged even the general and secret voting rights and thus anticipated them even on a political level by almost half a century, has lasted, although it is surely not easy to manage a collective of individualists like we have with the Vienna Philharmonic." Probably every Orchestra Chair in history would sign this last statement!

A Safety Net in the Opera

An 1865 survey yielded this statement, "that the splendid institution of the opera orchestra, the pearl of our opera theater, is paid very little." However, not until 1872 did Kaiser Franz Joseph I. see fit to approve a "Pension Institute for the k. k. Hof-Opern-Theater." At last, in September 1886, the "Verein Nicolai, Kranken-Kassa der Mitglieder des k. k. Hofopern-Orchesters" (Nicolai Association, a Health Insurance Company for the Members of the Imperial and Royal Court Opera Orchestra) was called into being, along with the Nicolai Concerts, to which, among others, Hans Richter, Johann Strauss and Gustav Mahler contributed generously.

Not until an agreement in 1953 did the State Opera legally recognize the existence of the Philharmonic. Paragraph 8 allows the orchestra members six weeks' leave during the season "in order to take part in the concert tours of the Vienna Philharmonic," and the Verein had to hire substitutes and remunerate them. Paragraph 9 required that "on the days preceding subscription concerts" there could be no obligatory rehearsal duty in the opera. With the Federal Theater Pension Law (1958) and the Orchestra Collective Contracts of 1969, 1983 and 2011, other cornerstones were laid: service limits for performances and rehearsals were sorted out, six Wagner operas (mentioned by name) of "overlong duration" were calculated as "double duty," and the "free allocation of service" or "rota" (the orchestra having autonomy in deciding which musicians are assigned to rehearsals and performances) was officially established. In 2007, the "Regulations on Orchestra Auditions" were set up.

It is a great jigsaw puzzle for the director of the State Opera to make arrangements for "his" orchestra. Dominique Meyer got to the heart of the 'director's nightmare:' "the orchestra is in Japan and I have all the great Wagner singers at my disposal—then what?"

Orchestral Expansions

The Philharmonic musicians are more than twice as strong today than they were in the year of their founding. In 1842, the opera orchestra comprised only 64 musicians, and by 1862, the year the subscription concerts were established, they were at 82. By the time of the move into the new opera house on the Ring in 1869, the group had grown to 100, and at the departure of Gustav Mahler in 1907, it was 120. After that, the number of Philharmonic musicians remained "frozen" until 1973. For a long time, the question of what to do with new members of the opera orchestra who wanted to join the Philharmonic Association (they were variously called "extraordinary members" in 1869, "Expectants" in 1903, and "Candidates" in 1971) had no satisfactory answer. "The conflict between the established members, who were hardly prepared to share their receipts, and their young colleagues would get sharper with every expansion of the orchestra." (Merlin)

In the post-war era, the continual increases in work outside the opera (Salzburg, concert tours, recording activity) were facing an orchestra "that was threatening to run out of breath," and the "lack of new recruits" was responsible (Merlin). With the controversial question of a reduction in the pension age came an unexpected request discovered by Christian Merlin in the archives: Violinist Theodor Hess petitioned for his pension, in order "to escape being persecuted by the lawyer of his divorced wife. As a pensioner, he would have to cede one third of his pension to his ex-wife, but he could keep any additional income for himself. So he hoped he would be able to play as a substitute in the orchestra." He accomplished this objective as well.

The most significant expansion of the opera orchestra since 1869 came about gradually, started by Böhm, and continued by his successors Karajan and Hilbert. By the year 1964 the State Opera orchestra counted 150, so thirty more than the Philharmonic! But that was only the beginning: "Between 1964 and 1970, 65 new members were taken on." (Merlin) The rule that was agreed upon after tough wrangling for the so-called "Expansion Generation" was: every Philharmonic candidate was obliged to a probationary period of three years before he could become a member of the Vienna Philharmonic—and the statutes were altered accordingly in 1973.

A wave of rejuvenation has taken place this century, since no less than 40% of the orchestra was pensioned between 2000 and 2012. Meanwhile, a noticeable "internationalization" has also developed, contradicting the prejudice that the orchestra is hermetically sealed. According to Merlin, there are orchestras "that have opened themselves up far less to the outside but have nonetheless been spared harsh criticism"—for instance, the

Staatskapelle Dresden consists of almost 92% Germans and the Mariinsky Orchestra of St. Petersburg does not have a single non-Russian player.

Two thirds of today's Philharmonic players come from Austria, one third from 22 countries, in which Merlin especially sees the comeback of the former "crown lands"—could this be the guarantee of an "Old Austrian" sound?

Audition

Now let us finally answer the title question of this chapter: the way leads only through the Vienna State Opera. There, in the Gustav Mahler Hall, the public drinks and chats while relaxing during the intervals. But whenever a member of the Philharmonic enters this room, inevitably his (or her) adrenalin level will rise as memories of *the* career moment are reawakened: this is where the auditions take place, the successful outcome of which is the prerequisite for acceptance into the opera orchestra.

A jury, comprised of the opera director and up to 25 members of the orchestra (especially from the instrument group for which a new recruit is sought), decides on the weal and woe of the applicants. To guarantee anonymity, they play behind a curtain. If the audition proves successful, the musician spends a probationary year in the opera orchestra, but is a member of the "Working Association of the Vienna Philharmonic" from the beginning and thus can be called up for concert service. After a three-year trial period in the opera and concert orchestras, a written application for membership in the *Verein der Wiener Philharmoniker* (the Association of the VPO) can be submitted and the decision is made at the next general meeting.

The most celebrated "failure" of the *Concurs*, as the audition was then called, was Fritz Kreisler, the master student of Joseph Hellmesberger, Jr. It is not known what wrecked his concertmaster career: the strong vibrato that he would have had to get rid of? Competitive jealousy from Rosé? It was he, at any rate, who attested that Kreisler could not sight-read. While these days, the pieces to be played are announced in advance, back then the candidates had to deal with music that they had never seen before—Kreisler, later the world famous virtuoso, had to play a complicated solo from Goldmark's *Queen of Sheba*.

Two sides of the audition: the loneliness of the applicant…

…and the multi-headed jury

Proud Vienna Philharmonic members from France: Violinist Isabelle Ballot and bassoonist Sophie Dartigalongue

Women? Women!

The young clarinetist Alfred Prinz' unusually long hair prompted this misperception from conductor Igor Markevitch: "That tall blonde there, she has no discipline!" he shouted in a rehearsal. No woman was admitted to the Philharmonic's ranks in Markevitch's lifetime (he died in 1983). Three years later, Herta and Kurt Blaukopf noted without further judgment: "There are no women Philharmonic members. Membership is reserved for the male sex, although even with the most careful reading of the association's rules, we could find no foundation for this privilege." At the 150-year anniversary of the orchestra in 1992, the mayor of Vienna, Helmut Zilk, spoke jocosely of a "male order", but other organizations, for instance the Austrian "Task Force for Women's Rights and Human Rights" and the American "National Organization for Women," could not see anything funny about the situation.

In 1963, the opera orchestra took its first female member: the American harpist Christine Anders, née Stavrache, was hired by opera director Karajan. During an acrimonious discussion at the *Hauptversammlung*, the harpist and harp teacher Hubert Jelinek put things this way: "sooner or later women will be coming, and you will just have to deal with that, as there are no male students in my class."

But it was Christine Anders' successor who became the first female regular member of the Philharmonic. Budapest native Anna Lelkes joined the opera orchestra in 1971 and in 1974, she joined the work group (*Arbeitsgemeinschaft*) of the Philharmonic. On February 27, 1997, the harpist became the first woman ever to join the Vienna Philharmonic as a regular member. A door had been opened; Chairman Werner Resel chose to pass through it in the opposite direction: he resigned "for personal reasons" five weeks later.

Polemical discussions about the presence of women in the orchestra went on for years, with the active involvement of the media, while a development was proceeding that is no longer a problem for a new generation. Harpist Charlotte Balzereit followed Lelkes in 2001, and in other instrument groups soon after that were: Ursula Ruppe, née Plaichinger (viola), Ursula Wex (cello) and Isabelle Ballot, née Caillieret (first violin). Since 2008, there has even been a concertmistress, Bulgarian native Albena Danailova.

The proportion of women in the Vienna Philharmonic is not comparable with that of orchestras who first took this path decades earlier. Thus, we find over 40% women in the New York Philharmonic and almost 39% in the Zürich opera house. Here is the current status of the other three Vienna orchestras: The Vienna Symphony Orchestra (founded in 1900) consists of over 20% of women, the Tonkünstler Orchestra of Lower Austria (founded in 1907) has a solid 50%, and the young ORF Radio Symphony Orchestra (founded in 1969) consists to one third of women. With a total of 142 seats, the Philharmonic has 16 women for the 2017/18 season, or over 11%, with one more, the solo flutist Silvia Careddu doing her trial year in the State Opera orchestra. At the Vienna Musikuniversität half of the younger cohort is female, as is the proportion of women auditioning for the State Opera orchestra—so the way is clear.

The first woman at the conductor's desk of the Philharmonic was not even our millennium's Simone Young, but Felix Weingartner's wife Carmen Studer, who led a concert in Salzburg. In the meantime, female conductors are no longer special in our orchestra; most recently, the French Emanuelle Haïm made her debut here with a Handel program in September 2016.

Social Responsibilities and Working with Youth

There have been benefit concerts given by the orchestra since early in its history. But in former days, the musicians were not wealthy: they had to struggle, and possibilities were limited. This has changed, and today opera salaries and concert fees are such that the orchestra can make donations to other causes as well. A few examples may suffice.

The orchestra bought and remodeled an inn in the Lower Austrian community of St. Aegyd for 250,000 euros, which was set aside for housing refugee families as of summer 2016. Additionally, 27 tickets for the New Year's Concert 2017 were auctioned off for the benefit of this house.

In the aftermath of the Fukushima nuclear disaster in March 2011, the "Vienna Philharmonic and Suntory Music Aid Fund Japan" was founded, for which over a million euros have been raised to date. Concerts, seminars and instrument donations at that time especially brought younger residents of the catastrophe region together.

Group portrait at the party for the fifth anniversary of the "Vienna Philharmonic and Suntory Music Aid Fund" in Suntory Hall, Tokyo

The Philharmonic Hous
in St. Aegyd

Young talents present themselves before the Summernight's Concert in 2016.

Oboist Wolfgang Plank and flutist Wolfgang Breinschmid in rehearsal and concert with young colleagues in Japan and Austria

The collaboration with "Superar" (an organization built on the model of the Venezuelan "El Sistema" for helping impoverished youth in Europe) culminated in a joint concert under Gustavo Dudamel at the start of 2017. Projects such as this interface social aid with youth development.

Our orchestra no longer sees itself as an elitist undertaking for well-off clients of middle age and older. Today, much time and money is invested in opening up to younger audiences. For quite some time now, the Philharmonic have acted as the godparents of the Vienna Music Gymnasium and most recently mounted several initiatives, for example the music appreciation program "password:Klassik," in the context of which "acoustic concert introductions" (*klingende Konzerteinführungen*), school concerts and workshops have been offered. In cooperation with the Salzburg Festival and with the support of the Salzburg Foundation of the American Austrian Foundation, they have also offered "password:Klassik" opera camps during the summer festival.

There is also emphasis on the promotion of young talent: namely the "International Orchestra Institute Attergau," the Angelika Prokopp Summer Academy under the artistic direction of bassoonist Michael Werba, and the "International Music Forum Trenta," with master courses for string players. "BePhilharmonic" is another successful youth program, for which the double bass player Christoph Wimmer initiated the "Strauss Contest 2016." It was financed by means of the Karajan Prize, which the Philharmonic won in 2014. Up-and-coming young ensemble players between six and nineteen were invited to send in music videos of the works of the Strauss dynasty. The winners gave a concert before the Sommernachtskonzert in 2016 in Schönbrunn, and Austrian television made a documentary about the project.

Behind the Scenes

The old song warns us: "Es kommt auf die Sekunde an bei einer schönen Frau," (With a beautiful woman, every second counts), and in this sense art is similar to love. "Was zählt, ist der Augenblick," (What counts is the moment): that is the title (borrowed from Nikolaus Harnoncourt) of the Philharmonic biography written by Franz Bartolomey. But it is easy to forget how much preparation has to precede the "moment." There is a great deal of organizational and practical work to be done beyond musical matters for a tour to take place, a concert to be staged, or a TV broadcast to be done.

The central managerial tasks are the responsibility of the administrative body known as the "Komitee." At the moment, it is made up of ten active members: the Chair and his deputy, the Business Manager, the treasurer, ticket manager, *Ordnungwahrer* (responsible for "order" in matters of discipline, dress, punctuality, etc.) are elected for three years each, and four members at large. The Chair represents the Verein externally and internally while the schedule dates—domestic as well as international—are managed by the Business Manager. The Komitee meets at least once a month, and the general assembly of the orchestra, which sets the general direction of the whole organization, meets annually and triennially elects the Komitee. Part of the Philharmonic's self-government are three other functionaries not on the Komitee: the Ball head, the head of the Historical Archive, and the tour leader.

"Self-government" for a long time meant that all the work would be done by active members of the Philharmonic themselves. But given the international scope of the demands on them, this is now longer thinkable. Nowadays, sixteen non-members of the orchestra are hired (three of them part-time) for the areas of general administration, artistic business office, public relations and communication, accounting, box office, music archives, historic archives and recording archives, where the acoustic treasures of the orchestra are preserved.

Further indispensable positions are the luthiers or violin makers (the Philharmonic mainly works with Wilfried Ramsaier-Gorbach, whose workshop is in the Musikverein building itself) and also three orchestra stage managers (*Orchesterwarte*), who have to take care of not just the State Opera and the Musikverein, but also all the other performance venues at home and abroad: and part of this includes transporting instruments, the setup and breakdown of chairs and stands, distributing and collecting the music materials.

Archival Work

Hardly any friends of music consider the organizational—and financial—services that are required to ensure that the right music scores are ready and available for each concert. This is the task of the music archive, founded in 1862. Its first librarian was violinist Carl Mayer, who wrote a letter to the committee asking for the acquisition of an appropriate music cabinet. If this was not possible, however, then the leadership of the archive could be "transferred to another member of the society" who "perhaps owned an appropriate cabinet for the purpose." In the time since then, the cabinet(s) have been taken care of—as has appropriate remuneration of the librarian. Once upon a time, the "Archiv-Cassa" ("archive fund") was financed through salary deductions levied upon musicians for disciplinary offenses. Payments were even made to the fund for minor offenses like being late for rehearsal. Even Felix Weingartner had to pay once when he didn't show up on time!

The archivist Franz Slavicek, who joined the orchestra in 1924 as a violist and was later principal second violin, catalogued and put the music holdings in order. In 1928, he found time for an intermezzo on the silver (silent) screen: because he had a resemblance to Franz Schubert, he was cast in a 1928 Hollywood film about the composer.

It is an aspect of a great tradition that our orchestra played Beethoven symphonies from music dating from the Nicolai era right into the new millennium. However, these precious documents have been kept in the Historical Archive since that time, which was first separated from the regular music library in 1979. A great event took place in early October of 2014, when the Vienna Philharmonic Orchestra was awarded the million-dollar Birgit Nilsson Prize. After a unanimous decision by the musicians, the prize money was used to expand the Historical Archive. In March 2017, it moved into its new quarters—but more of that in the final chapter.

Andreas Lindner and Florian Wieninger take care of the orchestra's treasury of music.

Nives Widauer's sculpture *Special Cases—Cosmic Rocket* in the Marble Hall of the Upper Belvedere

An International Orchestra

Today and Tomorrow

Since the end of the Second World War, the Vienna Philharmonic has performed abroad more than one thousand times. The reason for this relatively late discovery of the orchestra's wanderlust is obvious: as an opera orchestra, they had to give first priority to their duties in the pit at the opera house.

Until the turn of the 20th century, travel was confined to excursions within the Danube monarchy. Gustav Mahler was the first to take the orchestra over the border: the Philharmonic made its debut in Paris in 1900. The orchestra made isolated trips to England (with Franz Schalk in 1906), to Munich in 1910 for the Richard Strauss Week, to Switzerland (1917) and Czechoslovakia (1921) during its summer breaks.

The "Roaring Twenties" were transformative years for our orchestra as well. Work in the media began, at first for radio and records, and travel became more frequent. While the "main forces" left for their first foreign tour in 1922 (to South America) under Felix Weingartner, those who stayed behind, and pensioners and substitutes, played Mozart operas and concert pieces at the first Salzburg Festival. The Philharmonic's natural talent for "bi-location" was born!

Wilhelm Furtwängler dominated the tours for two decades. One early high point was the trip to Germany and London in April 1930 (in the middle of the opera season). He also had to lead most of the propaganda-oriented concerts that started immediately after the *Anschluss*. In the postwar period, the Philharmonic served as the ambassador of free Austria: first the France tour in March 1947 with Josef Krips and Paul Paray, then the Edinburgh tour with Bruno Walter, who said the Philharmonic had "fulfilled a very great mission. They showed Edinburgh and the world that this Vienna still lives and cannot die." In 1950, the orchestra traveled not only to Scandinavia with Furtwängler, but also to Egypt with Clemens Krauss, a trip that 85 musicians took part in, even if the advertisement

تيـــاترو محمـــد على

Théâtre MOHAMED ALY

Téléphone No. 25106

Sous le Haut Patronage de S.M. le Roi

WIENER PHILHARMONIKER

avec 97 Professeurs

sous la Direction du

Prof. CLEMENS KRAUSS

ORDRE DES CONCERTS

MARDI 21 FÉVRIER 1950 à 9 h. 30 p.m. (1er Concert)

SCHUBERT .... : Symphonie h-moll *(Inachevée)*
STRAUSS .... : Don Juan
Pause
BEETHOVEN........... : V. Symphonie *(Héroique)*

MERCREDI 22 FÉVRIER 1950 à 9 h. 30 p.m. (2e Concert)

WEBER.................. : Oberon Ouverture
PAGANINI .... : Moto perpetue
ENESCU .... : Rumânische Rapsodie
Pause
BEETHOVEN .... : VI. Symphonie *(Pastorale)*
Leonore III.

LUNDI 6 MARS 1950 à 6 h. 15 p.m. (3e Concert)

BRAHMS .... : I. Symphonie
Pause
H. WOLF............... : Italienische Serenade
STRAUSS .... : Till Eulenspiegel
WAGNER............... : Meistersinger

MARDI 7 MARS 1950 à 6 h. 15 p.m. (4e Concert)

DUKAS .... : Zauberlehrling
TSCHAIKOVSKY .... : V. Symphonie e-moll
Pause
MOZART .... : Jupiter Symphonie

JEUDI 9 MARS 1950 à 6 h. 15 p.m. (5e Concert)

SCHUBERT .... : Rosamunden Ouverture
TEO BERGER .... : Legende von Prinz Eugen
J. STRAUSS............ : Kaiserwalzer
Pause
J. STRAUSS............ : Czardas aus Ritter Pazman
JOH. U. JOS. STRAUSS : Pizicatto Polka
J. STRAUSS............ : Perpetum Mobile
Ouverture Fledermaus.

Publicity poster for the Egyptian tour in 1950—
with a slight exaggeration…

poster grandly announced “97 Professors!” Beginning in 1953, the collective contract with the opera enabled orchestra members to take six weeks’ leave of absence, thus opening the door to more travel opportunities. The first Japan tour was done under Paul Hindemith’s leadership. This was essentially a kind of trial balloon with an orchestra of only 52 men. Just as they had celebrated crossing the equator on their ocean voyage three decades earlier, this time they celebrated their first flight over the North Pole: they “paid tribute to their pioneering accomplishment by dropping a red-white-red flag over the North Pole.” (Blaukopf) It was an equally pioneering accomplishment when the Philharmonic played Bruckner in the USA for the first time in 1956. At the conductor’s desk was Carl Schuricht, who only ten years before had made his debut conducting Bruckner with the Philharmonic at the Salzburger Festival—at the age of 66! (Even more impressive in this respect: the Philharmonic debut of the Swedish conducter Herbert Blomstedt in 2011 at age 83!)

Travel activities from the mid-1950s on were dominated by three conductors, who in this sense as well followed in the footsteps of the “secret chief conductor” of the 30s to the 50s. Hellsberg reels off the “Big Four” in one breath: “Furtwängler, Böhm, Karajan and Bernstein were [...] more than ‘just’ conductors of an absolutely special class [...] but rather they were the manifestation of a whole generation’s outlook on life.” With Furtwängler’s death in 1954, the Philharmonic entered into a new phase of its history.

Karl Böhm

“As an anti-star, he came to have timeless greatness,” as Hellsberg asserts. Böhm was a short-term opera director (1955/56) until he made the uncareful remark that he did not want to sacrifice his international career to the State Opera, which led to his resignation. But in the concert world, he remained a dominating personality: the record lists 56 subscription concerts and 18 Nicolai concerts, concerts at the Salzburg Festivals and more than forty tours—the Japan tours under Karl Böhm became an especially loved tradition. On top of that are numerous records, TV and movie recordings—the last of which was of *Elektra*, completed just before his death in 1981.

If you include Böhm's opera evenings in Vienna and Salzburg, then his own estimate of having conducted the Philharmonic 1000 times was probably accurate. "His" orchestra thanked him with the Nicolai Medallion, the Ring of Honor, an Honorary Membership, the Schalk Medallion and in 1967, he was named Honorary Conductor.

Herbert von Karajan

Böhm's successor at the State Opera, who ran the house from 1956 to 1964, was even less interested in sacrificing his career to the house—on the contrary, he made it the base camp of his "empire." Still, the year he took office (1956), Karajan was made chief conductor of the Berlin Philharmonic "for life" and artistic director of the Salzburg Festival.

Hellsberg characterizes him as "the symbol of the *Wirtschaftswunder* (tr.: the economic "miracle" of the post war recovery), with all its positive and negative sides." Karajan never shied away from confrontation: In 1957, Karajan decided to bring the Berlin Philharmonic into the Salzburg Festival in addition to the Viennese Philharmonic, who had had a monopoly on it until then. The Viennese could not take part in the Salzburg Easter Festival, which Karajan founded in 1967, because of their opera duties; so the Berliners were the logical alternative, even without any opera experience. But at this point, Karajan had already left the Vienna Opera in anger. He took his leave in 1964 with a performance of *Frau ohne Schatten*, but he bridged over his years of Vienna "abstinence" with regular collaborations with the Philharmonic in Salzburg.

The reconciliation with Vienna came gradually in the mid-70s, culminating with a "Karajan-Stagione" at the State Opera. After Böhm's death, Karajan celebrated his comeback at the subscription concerts. "These final 'honeymoon' years reached their highpoint with the unforgettable New Year's Concert of 1987" (Merlin); and another high point was the *Coronation Mass* by Mozart in 1985 in St. Peter's Basilica. In February of 1989, Karajan was the star of the first "Vienna Philharmonic Week" in New York. He died in July of that year.

Aside from the last New York trip, two tours under Karajan stand out. Their world tour of 1959 took the orchestra to Japan, the US, and to such unusual destinations as Canada, India, the Philippines, Honolulu and Hong Kong. Equally successful was a tour of the Soviet Union and Scandinavia in 1962. On March 28 of that same year, the orchestra celebrated its 120th birthday in Leningrad. Just as Gustav Mahler had become more approachable on the Paris tour of 1900, so these trips abroad brought—temporarily—a "spring thaw" with Karajan.

But it was only in old age that the once aloof maestro became "kinder and gentler." Hellsberg passes along this pleasant story: "Once, when the overly brash entrance of one section leader of a Philharmonic string group disturbed Karajan's musical sensitivities, his reaction was not a bit impatient. 'Did you hurt yourself?' he asked, seemingly concerned, and the musicians' unrestrained laughter showed that criticism without attacking is the best and most liberating solution."

Leonard Bernstein

Through nearly a quarter century, the Philharmonic was associated with perhaps the last universal musical genius, the conductor, pianist, composer and teacher Leonard Bernstein. Whenever he came, his visits were planned with military precision down to the last detail, namely: "a several weeks long series of concerts, TV and recording sessions in Vienna, each of which was followed by an extended tour" (Hellsberg).

The kick-off event was his State Opera debut on March 16, 1966, with the premiere of *Falstaff*. Like so many other conductors before and after him, he was not comfortable with the free rotation schedule of the musicians (also known as the *Orchesterradel,* or "orchestra wheel"). Helmut Wobisch, the Business Manager, tried to make the situation more appetizing for him: "They all want to play under your direction, and we don't want to deprive anyone." Bernstein answered: "You are the smoothest-talking *gonef* (Yiddish: rascal) I know!"

At the beginning of April came two additional subscription concerts and a guest performance in Monte Carlo. In an irresistible gesture of modesty, the famous musician turned to the Philharmonic players and said: "This is *your* Mozart. You must tell me how to play him." In 1979, after a concert in Paris, Bernstein gave the orchestra an unabashed declaration

The anti-star: Karl Böhm

The superstar:
Herbert von Karajan

Musician of the heart: Leonard Bernstein

(1)

HÔTEL DE CRILLON
10 PLACE DE LA CONCORDE
PARIS
TÉLÉPHONE 296-10-81
TÉLÉGR. CRILONOTEL-PARIS 123
TELEX 290 204 CRILLON

An alle meine Collegen der Wienerphilharmoniker:

Brüder!

Ich kann mich nicht erinnern an eine höhere Sternstunde als die die wir zusammen mit der Neunte Beethoven musiziert haben.

Herzlichsten Dank!

5 Sept '79 Leonard Bernstein

…and his "love letter" to his "brothers"

of his love (see illustration, previous page: "To my colleagues of the Vienna Philharmonic: Brothers!").

There is a kind of "century story" attached to Bernstein's Philharmonic debut in 1966, going back to 1915. Gustav Mahler's *Das Lied von der Erde* was on the program—incidentally also a first time for Bernstein. The scores used were the same ones that Bruno Walter had used at the world premiere with the Vienna Philharmonic in 1915. Somewhat later, Bernstein conducted the work in New York as well. The score he used was that same score of Bruno Walter's, which he had, well, lovingly "adopted." The precious document stayed in New York until the beginning of 2017, when Barbara Haws, the chief archivist of the New York Philharmonic, brought it back to Vienna in March for the 175th birthday of our orchestra. "It's not a birthday without a present," she laughed, giving the score to Philharmonic Chair Andreas Großbauer.

Whether Bernstein was really the "most telegenic of all maestros," as Christian Merlin suggests, is questionable in light of Karajan's incredibly detailed and precisely planned self-marketing. But the statement that Bernstein "taught the orchestra how to play Mahler again,"—despite much previous Mahler programming under conductors like Klemperer, Walter, Furtwängler, Kubelik, Krauss, Böhm, Mitropoulos, Karajan, Solti and Abbado in the decades after 1945—is absolutely accurate.

Let us look at their travel activities with Hellsberg: "In the years 1987 to 1990 alone, the 'Viennese' gave 34 concerts abroad under Bernstein, which make him the most important tour conductor in the orchestra's history." Bernstein said farewell in the second "Vienna Philharmonic Week" in Carnegie Hall in March 1990. He was never able to accept the key role in the 150-year jubilee of the orchestra in 1992 that had been planned for him: Leonard Bernstein died in October 1990, one year after Karajan.

"The Moderns? I will have to learn them first…"

Gerhard Bronner wrote this text for his cabaret number *Der Karajanuskopf* (to the melody of Figaro's entrance aria in *The Barber of Seville*): "The moderns? First I'll have to learn them, and I don't have time today…" But that would be doing the great man an injustice. It is almost totally forgotten that under Karajan's aegis at the Salzburg Festival, a new opera was performed almost every summer. Karajan now and then brought new works into the Philharmonic repertory as well, such as Béla Bartók's *Music for Strings, Percussion and Celesta* in 1948. Furtwängler also conducted Bartók in addition to Korngold (the *Serenade for Strings*) and Paul Hindemith (*Symphonic Metamorphoses* 1947), *The Harmony of the World* 1953).

Hindemith himself made multiple appearances as director of the orchestra as well as at a new series of "Composers' Concerts" at the beginning of the 1960s. There was a need to catch up on things "modern," and gradually, composers like Aram Khatchaturian, Werner Egk, Boris Blacher, Hindemith, Benjamin Britten, Frank Martin and Wolfgang Fortner came to conduct their own works and those of others. Austrian contemporaries were also taken account of, among others Alfred Uhl and Anton Heiller. Gottfried von Einem found his way into the Philharmonic repertory with his *Philadelphia Symphony* under Georg Solti in November 1961. (Einem's opera *Danton's Death* had already been premiered in Salzburg in 1947.) Theodor Berger's works, among others, were conducted by Horst Stein.

One of the most influential composers of his time, Pierre Boulez, first worked with our orchestra during the Salzburg festival in the summer of 1962. He led works of Stravinsky in productions of Maurice Béjart's "Ballet of the XXth Century." Moderns, Mahler and Bruckner were the main focus of his regular collaboration with the Philharmonic, which began only in 1992 and ended in 2012. On the occasion of his eightieth birthday, Pierre Boulez was made an honorary member of the orchestra, which is indebted to him for (among other works) the first Philharmonic performance of Schönberg's piano concerto op. 42 with Daniel Barenboim in the same year and for the world premiere of Olga Neuwirth's *miramondo multiplo for Trumpet and Orchestra* in 2006 and for the world premiere of Jörg Widmann's *Armonica* in 2007. Boulez was, as violinist Helmut Zehetner remembers, not only a conductor with an amazing memory, but also a "kindly older gentleman in whom one would never have suspected the revolutionary of his earlier years." While Clemens Hellsberg complained that Boulez' works were still missing from the orchestra's repertory in his standard history of the orchestra, *Demokratie der Könige* (1992), this has happily changed for the better. A recent example: at the 38th Music Festival in the Wiener Konzerthaus in 2017 the Philharmonic presented *Notations* with Barenboim as a conductor.

The Vienna Philharmonic are not modern "specialists," but of course they do play the music of the 20th and 21st centuries. At the Salzburg Festival in the summer of 2017, the orchestra accompanied not only the "Netrebko-*Aida*," but also prominently featured—staying with opera—Shostakovich's *Lady Macbeth of Mtsensk*, Berg's *Wozzeck* and Aribert Reimann's *Lear*. Andreas Großbauer was satisfied: "I enjoy seeing the Vienna Philharmonic dealing with the conflicting priorities of tradition and innovation." And even Karl Böhm appealed to the open-mindedness of the audience with his address on the 125th anniversary of the orchestra in 1967: "Don't let your subscription lapse when a work is on the program by a composer who lived, or could have lived, in this century!"

Sometimes "New Guys" become Honorary Members

Zubin Mehta came to Vienna to study as an 18-year-old and fell in love immediately: "Because I wanted to become a conductor, the Philharmonic was my barometer, my axiom, my everything." On June 11, 1961, he gave his Philharmonic debut as a last-minute substitute for Eugene Ormandy, and the program was repeated at his 50-year jubilee in June 2011 at the Nicolai Concert. The Vienna Festival Weeks in 1962 and the Salzburg Festivals of 1962 and 1963—these were the "trial passages" the young Indian had to go through before being invited to conduct his first subscription concert. Since then, Zubin Mehta has become one of the busiest and most highly esteemed conductors of the Philharmonic: he was made an honorary member in 2001. He had a late debut in December 2016: during the rehearsal period for *Falstaff* at the State Opera, he conducted (Haydn and Mozart) in the Hofmusikkapelle for the first time.

Lorin Maazel, too, (an honorary member since 2007, deceased in 2014) owed his Philharmonic debut to a last-minute substitution for Karajan in 1962. His connection to the orchestra became closer during his short directorship of the State Opera (1982-1984), after which a little "ice age" began with Vienna. 1991 saw Maazel stage his comeback as Philharmonic subscription conductor after four and a half years' absence, and in that same year, he led a concert performance of *Elektra* in Carnegie Hall. As a successor to Willi Boskovsky, he conducted the New Year's Concert eleven times between 1980 and 2005. There is a DECCA CD box, *Lorin Maazel in Vienna,* which documents that collaboration with music of Tchaikovsky, Sibelius, and Richard Strauss.

An "interrupted love story" connected the Philharmonic with Georges Prêtre: a story that began with his filling in for Knappertsbusch in 1963, was picked up again in Salzburg in 1989 and was capped off by two New Year's Concerts and an honorary membership (2010) for the conductor and ended with his death in early 2017. The Frenchman once said: "I play the most beautiful instrument there is: the orchestra," a compliment that the "Viennese" could certainly take personal pride in.

The late (2014) Claudio Abbado did not attain the rank of Honorary Member. In 1965, he debuted as a Philharmonic conductor at the Salzburg Festival playing Mahler, his first subscription concert took place in January 1967. Up until 1997, he led the orchestra more than 500 times, often on international tours as well as at the State Opera, for which he was the music director in the second half of the 1980s.

Daniel Barenboim also made his debut with the Vienna Philharmonic in Salzburg in 1965—but at the piano. Not until 1989 did his time come as a Philharmonic conductor, and only in 1991 in the subscription series. He has returned over and over, occasionally combining the roles of conductor and soloist, to the desk of the Philharmonic, whose New Year's concerts he has directed twice. Barenboim, chief conductor of the Staatskapelle Berlin for life, once said something about the Philharmonic that might not please other orchestras: "It's like a miracle. I come to them and can start at a place where I stopped with others. It's as if they had direct contact to the music: it must have something to do with the air...or with the Wiener Schnitzel—I can't say!"

Seiji Ozawa first came to the Salzburg Festival podium in 1966 ("Karajan urged me to conduct this orchestra"). Back then, he could only dream about the honorary membership he would receive one day (2010) and he did not direct his first subscription concert until 1990. He did not

From left to right: Lorin Maazel, Pierre Boulez, Georges Prêtre

NIKOLAUS HARNONCOURT
PIARISTENGASSE 38/8
A-1080 WIEN

LOHEN 1
A-4880 ST. GEORGEN i.A.

4. Dez. 2015

Liebe Philharmoniker,
lieber Herr Großbauer,
lieber Herr Krumpöck,

ich bin gezwungen, mein musikalisches Auftreten in dieser Saison zu beenden – ich bin an meine körper= lichen Grenzen gestoßen. Unser Mendelssohn-Konzert in der Salzburger Mozartwoche ist mir also unmöglich.

Hier ist nicht der Ort, unsere großartige, langjährige spannende Zusammenarbeit zu beleuchten.

herzlichst und dankbar
Ihr
[signature]

P.S.: die Unvollendete aus Berlin klingt mir ewig weiter....

Farewell letter from Nikolaus Harnoncourt

Dimitri Mitropoulos

os Kleiber and Riccardo Muti, Christian Thielemann opens the Philharmonic Ball.

introduce himself at the Vienna State Opera until May 18, 1995, where he was appointed Music Director in 2002. When he took the position, he held a press conference in which he gave his surprising reason for taking the opera job: "I like boys," he said quite distinctly, although it turned out he was misheard: he said "voice," not "boys," and was just confessing to his love of singing. The New Year's Concert conducted by Seiji Ozawa in 2002 is a front runner even today in CD and DVD sales.

Riccardo Muti debuted with the Philharmonic in Salzburg in 1971 with *Don Pasquale* and introduced himself to the Vienna State Opera with *Aida* two years later. On this occasion he also conducted the opening of the Philharmonic Ball. In the spring of 1975, he and Karl Böhm undertook a tour of Japan, and Muti led his first subscription concert in 1975. The maestro will conduct the New Year's Concert for the fifth time in 2018. Muti, an honorary member of not just the Philharmonic but also of the Vienna Hofmusikkapelle, scatters roses: "I love the Vienna Philharmonic, and they have continuously been "my" orchestra for over 45 years. I admire their musicality, nobility, elegance, and their inspired playing. My bond with these extraordinary musicians has enriched my life, in both the human and artistic sense."

The "difficult" Carlos Kleiber first conducted at the State Opera in 1973 (*Tristan und Isolde*) and in the following year conducted the Philharmonic for the first time in a guest appearance in Bratislava. In 1979, he conducted the first of only eight subscription concerts. Still, the orchestra is indebted to him for two impressive New Year's Concerts (1989 and 1992) and also for anecdotes like this one: during rehearsals of Beethoven's 4th Symphony Kleiber implored the musicians to play an accompaniment figure in the Adagio as if they were singing "Theres." "You play 'Marie' instead of 'Theres,'" he told them, enraged, and a smart remark from the orchestra annoyed Kleiber so much that he just walked out. Lorin Maazel, taking over, told them, "Now please don't play neither 'Marie' nor 'Theres,' but Maazel!"

The great Austrian conductor Nikolaus Harnoncourt first crossed paths with the Philharmonic on December 8, 1984, at a point when he had made a name for himself as a pioneer of "original" sound. Twenty years later to the day, he was made an honorary member of the orchestra. His collaboration with the orchestra resulted in memorable performances of Mozart and Beethoven, but also of Dvořák, Smetana and Berg, and the same is true of the New Year's Concerts of 2001 and 2003 that Harnoncourt conducted. He put aside all his duties as a conductor in December of 2015 and died in March of 2016.

There is not enough space to discuss so many other conductors, but a few should at least be mentioned: the Italians Carlo Maria Giulini and Giuseppe Sinopoli, the Korean Myung-Whun Chung, the chief conductor designate of the Metropolitan Opera Yannick Nézet-Séguin…and Dimitri Mitropoulos, who died too young. Even his very first concert rehearsal in Salzburg in 1954 brought with it a flattering surprise: the Greek with the photographic memory already knew all the musicians' names at sight: he had memorized them the night before. Mitropoulos always conducted from memory, as with *Elektra* at the Salzburg Festival. Once, during the rehearsal of the complicated work, he closed his eyes to think a bit, and one Philharmonic member whispered to another: "Now he's turning the page!" It was not just Mitropoulos' intellectual and artistic capacity that impressed the orchestra, but also his modesty and kindness. Once he said this to the Philharmonic violinist Erich Graf: "Even before I learned to play my first notes, I learned to love people."

Does the Philharmonic need a Conductor?

After mentioning all these great conductors by name, this question may not seem serious, but „the idea that the orchestra basically doesn't need a conductor remains deeply anchored in the mentality of the Philharmonic" (Merlin).

The somewhat vulgar comparison with a prophylactic ("without is nicer, but with is safer") and jokey remarks about less talented "repertory conductors" ("he gave the downbeat and from then on gave no more appreciable resistance") come to mind. The threat "we just play as he directs" was once turned around in a complimentary way by no other conductor than Wilhelm Furtwängler. He loved doing the *Kaiserwalzer* as an encore without being a particular expert in the music of Johann Strauss. One evening, the musicians decided on their own to give the interpretation a little more *Schwung* and not to follow the somewhat broad tempi of the master. When one musician asked if Furtwängler was happy with the evening's *Kaiserwalzer* after the concert, the conductor answered, "Excellent! I directed as you played."

Furtwängler's work was always particularly valued by the orchestra, precisely because he was far from any kind of "mathematical" beating of the rhythm. One anecdote that is all too familiar—and probably just a good invention—is this one: a Berlin and a Vienna Philharmonic member are talking about how they each know when to come in, given Furtwängler's cramped, wavy gesturing while conducting. The Berliner: "We wait until his baton has reached the level of the second button on his tuxedo and forms a right angle to the desk…and when do you come in?" and the Viennese says: "When we get sick of waiting!"

There were often moments when prominent guest conductors would flirt with their "superfluousness" and give the orchestra its head. This happened with Richard Wagner's guest performance of *Lohengrin* at the Vienna Court Opera in 1876. In the postlude to the duet of Ortrud and Elsa, according to cellist Sulzer's account, "Wagner laid his baton on the desk, let the orchestra play on alone, smiling to himself about publicly showing his great confidence in the orchestra this way." When the postlude was over, there was such a storm of applause that Wagner had to stop, get up and acknowledge the audience. Then he turned to the musician sitting next to him and said, 'It looks to me like the audience likes it better when I *don't* conduct!'"

Hugo Burghauser reports an episode that shows something of Richard Strauss' feel for psychology. During a rehearsal, there were repeated problems with a certain entrance. Strauss said to the musicians: "I know, it's usually the *Kapellmeister*," and he asked the orchestra to play without him—and the entrance was perfect! Burghauser: "Obviously, it was the increased concentration of all the players as soon as they knew they were doing it on their own."

One YouTube hit is the short film by the Wiener Musikverein in which Leonard Bernstein does…*not*…conduct Haydn. In the finale of Symphony No. 88, he cues the downbeat and then does little more than wiggle his

eyebrows, nod his head, and shrug his shoulders. Though this might be plausible in a symphony movement with a steady tempo, it would be quite risky in the opera. "He draws on his advance of trust in the musicians in a breathtaking way," remembered Franz Bartolomey. In the third act of *Rosenkavalier*, he merely signals the downbeat and does not conduct at all after that. He just barely moves his shoulders—and that in such a tricky piece where so many very small parts are interwoven together. I have never seen the orchestra concentrate that hard—before or after."

Simon Rattle called for a similar *coup de main* in Tokyo in 2001—again Bartolomey's account of it: "At the beginning of the encore, one of the op. 46 *Slavonic Dances*, he just cues the orchestra's entrance, sticks his baton into the concertmaster's music and walks calmly to the timpani in the back. Our timpanist makes room for him and Simon plays them perfectly to the end. The audience roars its approval."

Once, during the encore portion of a waltz concert in London under Boskovsky, the orchestra's New Year's prankster Franz Broschek gave his own (unauthorized) cue: the conductor had not come back on stage yet, and when Broschek sounded his little drum, the orchestra understood and started playing the *Radetzky March* on its own! In 2014 at the Musikverein, Daniel Barenboim still cued the downbeat for that same obligatory encore and then, after shaking the hands of all the musicians, slipped off stage. No question, however, that he had implemented his personal intentions in all the waltzes and polkas that had gone before—and of course this is the case with all famous conductors. Even if it can be nicer "without," it is significantly more interesting "with."

The special case of having two conductors on the podium at once occurred in October 2016 in Tokyo's Suntory Hall: the *Thunder and Lightning* Polka under Zubin and Seiji had a unique value.

Philharmonic Players as Conductors

Even aside from personalities like Hans Richter and Arthur Nikisch, Philharmonic players have repeatedly left the orchestra to become conductors. Here are some examples: Emil Paur joined the orchestra as a first violin in 1872 at the age of 17. In 1875, he left voluntarily to pursue his ambitions. These led him to the top positions at the Boston and Pittsburgh Symphony Orchestras as well as the New York Philharmonic, with whom he led the American premiere of Strauss' *Ein Heldenleben* in 1902. Rudolf Nilius, a former Philharmonic cellist, distinguished himself in the 1920s as a recording conductor.

Concertmaster Walter Weller switched to a conducting career after filling in once for Karl Böhm, as did Erich Binder later: in 1981 he subbed, without a rehearsal, for Christoph von Dohnányi in Stravinsky's *Rite of Spring*. Manfred Honeck, too, brother of concertmaster Rainer Honeck, gave up his seat in the viola section for a career which eventually made him music director of the Pittsburgh Symphony Orchestra in 2008. And Johannes Wildner went from his position as Philharmonic second violin to an internationally sought conductor.

At Home Abroad

The great tradition of concert tours in the USA and Japan, with hundreds of concerts dating back to 1956, cannot be examined here in detail: South Korea also is a country regularly visited by the Philharmonic.

It is substantially easier to get an overview of the orchestra's presence in China. The Karajan tour of 1959 was not repeated until April 1973: following a Korean and Japanese tour, the orchestra played in Beijing under Claudio Abbado at the express wish of the Austrian government—with a state subsidy, as well.* Between then and 1995, the Philharmonic then gave nine more concerts in Hong Kong—under André Previn and James Levine. In the next two decades, with Mehta, Ozawa, Gergiev, Eschenbach, Thielemann, Buchbinder and Dudamel, the orchestra's visits to China were done as "appendices" to the Japan or Korean tours. The appearances planned for fall 2017, in Shenzhen, Guanghou, Shanghai, Nanjing and Macao and with Andris Nelsons are the Philharmonic's first independently organized

* Public support for travel has only seldom been granted to the Philharmonic, among others for the Paris tour in 1900 and concert tours in the First and Second World Wars.

trips to China. It is a market of hope, as Andreas Großbauer remarked on a promotional tour with a chamber music ensemble: "I have never seen so many young people at a concert as I have in China."

Australia was the latest continent to be "discovered" by the Philharmonic. The first concerts in Sydney were given in September 2006 under the leadership of Valery Gergiev, and these were followed by appearances with Christoph Eschenbach in October 2011 in Perth, Brisbane, and Sydney again.

In addition, two special moments from the more recent history of the Philharmonic with Japan and the USA, respectively, should be mentioned. In October of 2016, Nobutada Saji, president of Suntory Hall, received the Franz Schalk Medallion in gold. This award has been given in Japan twice before: in 1973 to Daigoro Arima, president of the NHK Orchestra, and in 1998 to Keizo Saji, the father and predecessor of the current awardee. In February of 2017, the "Vienna Philharmonic Society" of New York held its first public function: the society held a fundraising reception with the collaboration of the Vienna Philharmonic, the proceeds from which will benefit the youth programs of the orchestra in New York.

The fact that the Vienna Philharmonic Orchestra is now an international orchestra is proven by the numbers, which have grown impressively. In the 1935/36 season the orchestra played 75 concerts, of which 38 were in Vienna, 34 at the Salzburg Festival, one more in the rest of Austria and two abroad. Half a century later, in 1985/86, the total number of concerts was 102, allocated thus: 33 in Vienna, 41 in Salzburg, 3 in the rest of Austria, 25 in the US, Japan, South America, Switzerland and Germany. In the 2015/16 season, of a total 138 concerts, 49 were abroad, 35 in Salzburg, six in other Austrian cities…and only 48 in Vienna. Thus, for the first time, the "Viennese" were heard more abroad than in their home town.

A "Media Orchestra"

The journey into the world of media, at first radio and phonograph records, began in the 1920s. Radio Wien began broadcasting on October 1, 1924, that winter, to be followed by a broadcast with the Philharmonic Sedlak-Winkler quartet. In the same year—the orchestra had to gather around an

So are the media a disturbance at concerts?

acoustic gramophone funnel to make its first record—first violinist Josef Klein conducted the *Blue Danube Waltz*.

"His Master's Voice" started its recording activities in the Mozart-Saal of the Wiener Konzerthaus with (among others) Franz Schalk, Bruno Walter, Clemens Krauss and Carl Alwin at the podium. In those days, there were no editing capabilities, a piece could only be recorded as a whole on wax plates. Witeschnik tells us of a recording of the *Freischütz* overture with Felix Weingartner conducting, which was first "torpedoed" by a horn "hiccup" and then by the clatter of a dropped clarinet mouthpiece. As time was getting short, they finally got a perfect recording. Overcome with relief, the conductor exclaimed right at the last measure: "This time nothing happened!", and with that the recording was dead.

In the 1920s, the public was still using crystal sets, even for live broadcasts from the Konzerthaus, the State Opera, and the Salzburg Festival. In 1926, an "open line" was set up between Vienna and Salzburg: three opera productions, one chamber music evening with the Rosé Quartet and one concert of the Philharmonic under Franz Schalk were made accessible to Vienna listeners. One more high point from 1931 on were the transcontinental broadcasts: for the first time, one could hear the Vienna Philharmonic live in the US.

Weingartner recorded all the Beethoven symphonies for Columbia; *Das Lied von der Erde* with Kerstin Thorborg and Charles Kullmann, led by its world premiere conductor Bruno Walter, was recorded live on fourteen record sides in May 1936 on the 25th anniversary of Mahler's death. Two years later, in January of 1938, the live recording of Mahler's Ninth under Bruno Walter marked an endpoint; he had to break off his recording of *Die Walküre* after the first act.

But recording activities did not cease, even when the opera itself closed in 1944. On the day after the Richard Strauss' 80th birthday, June 12, 1944, the orchestra's last collaboration took place with the composer recording some of his own orchestral works. Although Herbert von Karajan was still under a work ban by the Allies in 1946, he was being promoted by Walter Legge, the legendary producer of EMI, and made recordings of Schubert, Beethoven, Brahms and Strauss (thus, a repertory that would have been allowed even before 1945) with the Philharmonic in the Musikverein.

Furtwängler gave the orchestra this written advice in August 1948: "If you are desired by everyone, [you can] adopt the same attitude I did in 1937, namely not to enter into *any* exclusive contracts." Nonetheless, the orchestra did conclude a long-term contract with DECCA in 1948. Their recording chief John Culshaw would go on to perform such meritorious service that the orchestra awarded him the Nicolai Medallion in 1959. Particularly the first complete recording of Wagner's *Ring des Nibelungen* under Georg Solti became a part of history. After intensive research, Culshaw advocated for the recordings using the Sofiensäle in Vienna. With his *Rheingold* in 1958, "a new chapter of recording history" (Blaukopf) had begun, and the acoustically overwhelming stereophonic recording was soon selling at the top of American sales lists. *Tristan und Isolde* followed under Solti in 1961, and the *Ring* was completed with *Siegfried* (1962), *Götterdämmerung* (1964) and *Die Walküre* (1965).

Generous investments (among other things in a 28-channel mixing console) made the Sofiensäle into a modern music studio, where orchestra rehearsals for the State Opera were also soon held. Culshaw intervened in matters regarding recording quality, spelling out to the board which musicians should or should not be involved, and "his demands were acceded to in all points," as Merlin reports. "This was the first time an outside person intervened in such a way in artistic decisions and particularly in casting questions, which the Philharmonic had denied even the conductor." This was only tolerated because recording had become an indispensable activity for the orchestra, artistically and commercially.

At Karajan's advice, the exclusive contract with DECCA was dissolved, and this gradually enabled the orchestra to make recordings with other firms: EMI, SONY and Deutsche Grammophon. Record contracts in the last third of the last century determined parts of the concert and travel schedule of the orchestra, but also made certain synergies possible: in 1971, a recording of *Der Rosenkavalier* was made under the direction of Leonard Bernstein in parallel with the performances he conducted at the State Opera. In September and October 1975, recordings of *Die Meistersinger von Nürnberg* were made in the Sofiensäle. While Sir Georg Solti was conducting here, Christoph von Dohnányi was simultaneously rehearsing the premiere of *Meistersinger* at the State Opera, which occurred on October 21!

The number of CD releases has meanwhile been sharply reduced: there is now more concentration (though not exclusively) on the New Year's and Summernight Concerts. Also, there is another annual CD release, the "Special Annual Edition": starting with Georges Prêtre (2013) through Christian Thielemann (2014), Lorin Maazel (2015), Riccardo Muti (2016) up to Mariss Jansons (2017), conductors with especially close bonds to the Philharmonic are given exemplary live recordings.

Some of the results of the cooperation with Deutsche Grammophon are contained in the lavish *175th Anniversary Edition*, 44 CDs with recordings that featured not just the "great oldies," but also put the focus on conductors such as John Eliot Gardiner, James Levine, André Previn, Claudio Abbado, Pierre Boulez and Christian Thielemann.

Getting the Picture

In 1948, the Philharmonic began to appear in audio-visual media with a series of short music films meant for the US and featuring conductors Krips and Böhm. This activity increased steadily into the 1960s thanks to the medium of television. The Philharmonic's connection to the production company UNITEL caused the general director of the Austrian Broadcasting Corporation (ORF) Gerd Bacher, to conclude a contract of cooperation with UNITEL, otherwise "the ORF would have simply had to forgo broadcasting the Philharmonic, which it did not understand to be part of its cultural mission." In 1983, the Philharmonic began its cooperation with the Telemondial firm, whose artistic director was Herbert von Karajan.

Even Leonard Bernstein said: "Be nice to UNITEL," and the friendship paid off. Around one hundred TV productions of the Vienna Philharmonic have been available at the classical music portal *myfidelio.at* since September 2016. This impressive program on the internet platform jointly operated by ORF and UNITEL extends from historic productions (the oldest is Furtwängler's Salzburg *Don Giovanni*) to live concerts shown as livestreams. Although Otto Strasser, back in 1981, quite rightly maintained that "records" (the CD had not yet been invented) and television were income sources that should not be underestimated, now presenters have to think about things completely differently. With "Fidelio" presentations, explained the intendant of the Musikverein Thomas Angyan, broadcasts have to be transferred from the debit to the credit side, that is, to the marketing budget: "Where we once could expect revenues, we now have to invest." The Philharmonic regularly now makes its subscription concerts available to the internet audience on the "Fidelio" platform (which charges fees).

Nonetheless, one special event that brings record CD sales and television viewers by the millions contributes immensely to the world renown of the Vienna Philharmonic.

The Myth of the New Year's Concert

The very first "New Year's concert" was actually held at the height of summer: On August 11, 1929, the young State Opera director Clemens Krauss conducted a Strauss-only program at the Salzburg Festival. A decade later, albeit on the last day of the year, the real birthday of the annual waltz and polka concert was fixed, again with Krauss conducting to mark the year's change.

Vienna would not be Vienna without a little joke or two, even with the war raging for the last four months. The last piece of the first section of the program was the Johann Strauss polka *The Hunt*, featuring quite audible gunshots. At the end, when Krauss was presented with a huge laurel wreath—there being no real laurel available—fashioned from preserved oak leaves, the violist Alfons Grünberg said to his desk-mate Ernst Morawec: "Krauss gets off his first shot—and already he's wearing oak-leaves."* As early as 1941—upon request from "higher up"—the orchestra gave a concert radiating "optimism" and "fun" to benefit the Nazi propaganda program "Strength through Joy."

In 1946 and 1947, before Clemens Krauss could return (his work ban was in effect until 1948), Josef Krips took over the New Year's concerts. Krauss' sudden death in May 1954 in Mexico (people wondered if a "broken heart" played a role here, due to being denied the directorship of the State Opera) left a gap that was not filled until after several votes at the orchestra's general meeting on November 25th, just five weeks before the first scheduled concert. The Chair Hermann Obermeyer thought, "Boskovsky should do it, from the podium." The concertmaster, who once had done his apprenticeship in the orchestra under Strauss' grandson Johann and who had an international reputation as a conductor of the lighter muse, was elected "provisory" conductor of the New Year's concerts. "Provisory" appointments often last a long time in Austria—in this case, a quarter of a century: Willi Boskovsky conducted the Philharmonic's New Year's Concert, violin in hand, from 1955 to 1979. He was followed by opera director designate Lorin Maazel. The New Year's Concert was in a way the last bastion of a "chief conductor"

* Oak leaves are a part of the Iron Cross medal, a high military decoration in Germany at the time of the Second World War.

Two New Year's Concerts: under Willi Boskovsky (right) and Riccardo Muti (below)

on Philharmonic territory: Maazel conducted the concert seven years in a row. Since 1987, the year of the legendary Karajan New Year's concert, the conductors have changed from time to time as well.

The event has been carried live on television since 1959 (in color since 1969) and has since grown to be the most recognized "classical" concert event in the world. Although in the jubilee year of 1992, "only" 42 stations in the whole world broadcast it on TV, the New Year's concert of 2017 (Gustavo Dudamel being the youngest conductor ever to conduct it) was broadcast to over 90 countries and watched by more than 50 million people. In 2015, the edition *Neujahrskonzert: Die gesamten Werke* was brought out, containing all 319 works that have been played since 1941 on 23 CDs.

The New Year's concerts not only provide the quality light music of the past with the "consecration" of a Philharmonic rendering, but we are also reminded every year of the once spontaneous (but now ritually regimented) excitement with which the fans of the "classics" used to greet their favorites: they can interrupt the *Blue Danube Waltz* with applause, and the finale, the *Radetzky March*, is accompanied by rhythmic clapping.

The Summernight's Concert

Since 2004, the New Year's Concert has had a summer supplement—even though the first few had weather more reminiscent of late fall. In May 2004, Bobby McFerrin conducted a "Concert for Europe" at the invitation of the Federal Government. While only 30,000 visitors were expected, no fewer than 90,000 actually flocked to the park of Schönbrunn Palace—an 'institution' was born. In 2005 (and 2015), Mehta was at the podium, and in 2006, the conducting tenor Plácido Domingo (along with his singing colleague Rolando Villazón) appeared. Rain forced a postponement, at which Juan Diego Flórez filled in as a soloist.

Valery Gergiev conducted the Philharmonic in 2007 (with 140,000 guests, a new audience record) and in 2011, this time to aid the victims of the Japanese earthquake: 60 television stations broadcast the event. Georges Prêtre led the concert in 2008, the first one to be called a "Summernight's Concert," and after him came Daniel Barenboim (2009), Franz Welser-Möst (2010), Gustavo Dudamel (2012), Lorin Maazel (2013),

Perhaps the world's most beautiful concert backdrop:
A Summernight's Dream at Schönbrunn

Christoph Eschenbach (2014 and 2017), and Semyon Bychkov (2016). This open-air event with Schönbrunn as a backdrop has meanwhile become established as the Philharmonic's calling card, but unlike the New Year's Concert, it is not a revenue bringing event but an investment in opening up new levels of audience. Over 100,000 in attendance, over half a million TV viewers in over 80 countries…in view of the publicity value for Vienna, there should be a few more public institutions sharing the costs of this expensive concert.

A "Ball Orchestra?"

Vienna has a particularly strong "ball" tradition. For more than a few, the Philharmonic Ball, once again a regular event since 1949, is the high point of the carnival season. The list of opening night directors reads like a "Who's Who" of the most important podium personalities, from Knappertsbusch to Sir Simon Rattle. The latter introduced himself with a compliment that goes beyond ball matters alone: "This orchestra knows how to dance." Zubin Mehta was not asked to conduct the opening until 1969, but he had already "misappropriated" the *Fanfare* Richard Strauss had written for the ball five years earlier in the new Dorothy Chandler Pavilion in Los Angeles.

In 1955, there were even two balls presented by the Philharmonic. In addition to the obligatory January date, they also gave a "Bal Paré" on November 5th following the festive reopening of the Vienna State Opera House.

With its increasing financial security, the orchestra could be more generous to external causes. Whereas the first Philharmonic Balls were originally to help their own charities, in recent years the ball committee has been donating to those in need: in 2015 for unaccompanied underage refugees in the "Sidra House," in 2016 for two mother-child shelter houses, in 2017 for the next generation of orchestra musicians, supporting the Angelika Prokopp Summer Academy of the Vienna Philharmonic. Starting in 2016, there has been a charity dinner for good causes before the ball.

On March 3, 2011, the Vienna Philharmonic entered a new phase of its "ball life:" at the invitation of the new State Opera director Dominique

Wilhelm Furtwängler conducting the opening of the Philharmonic Ball (1950)

Meyer, they played at the opening of the Vienna Opera Ball (conducted by Music Director Welser-Möst) for the first time. And when our orchestra played at the Ball Opening Night in 2017 under the leadership of a woman (Speranza Scappucci), it did not strike anyone as "exotic."

Jubilee Year 2017

On the last day of the old year, in the context of the "Silvesterkonzert" on December 31, 2016, the former federal president Dr. Heinz Fischer was named a "Patron" of the Vienna Philharmonic. Meanwhile, it appears that he is only the first of a growing network of cultural ambassadors in several countries: in the summer of 2017, the former UN Secretary-General Ban Ki-moon was also named a Philharmonic patron.

The New Year's Concert of the year 2017 was also the occasion for new clothing for the orchestra: for their jubilee, the Philharmonic ordered the "Philharmonic Suit," a newly designed concert outfit for men and women created by legendary British designer Vivienne Westwood and Andreas Kronthaler. Since then, it has been discovered that errors were made in taking measurements and that it will probably be a little longer before the new costuming project is completed. But what already seems to fit perfectly is the statement made by designer Westwood on the occasion of presenting the suits: "An orchestra may be the highest achievement of the human race." But she also broke a lance for tradition in the same breath: "If one destroys tradition, one has nothing to build up."

One good tradition since the 150th jubilee of the Vienna Philharmonic is the coin named after them. In 2017, the new 20-euro silver coin marked "*175 Jahre Wiener Philharmoniker*" with portraits of founders Nicolai, Schmidt and Becher on one side, and a section from Max Oppenheimer's painting "*Das Orchester*" (see pages 64–65) on the other.

"Two Philharmonics"

As they had been founded in the same year, at the beginning of 2017, the Vienna and New York Philharmonics decided to share one part of their celebration with each other. Thus, the exhibition *Vienna and New York: 175 Years of Two Philharmonics* traveled from the Austrian Cultural Forum New York to the Vienna Haus der Musik, where, on the orchestra's jubilee day, March 28, the exhibition was ceremoniously opened under the title *2x 175 Jahre Philharmoniker* (2 x 175 Years of the Philharmonic). Chair Andreas Großbauer: "This is one more opportunity to celebrate without always just saying: 'Us, us, us!'

Attending were among others honorary members Christa Ludwig and Rudolf Buchbinder, former Chairs Walter Barylli, Werner Resel and Clemens Hellsberg, who celebrated his own 65th birthday on the same day. Or, as Heinz Fischer put it: "He chose the 110th birthday of the Vienna Philharmonic to come into the world."

On that day, the Historical Archive of the orchestra officially moved into its new quarters—actually just an in-house move on the same floor of the Haus der Musik, but into a generous 4000 square feet. At last there is room for their precious holdings and also for visiting scholars to dig into the history of this orchestra. Archive head Wolfgang Plank, Silvia Kargl and Friedemann Pestel displayed treasures from the New York and Vienna collections (to which, as mentioned, the score of *Das Lied von der Erde* has indeed been returned).

In one of the reading rooms, one's eyes and ears can be astounded by *The 175*, a hand-crafted record player that the "Pro-Ject Audio Systems" firm dedicated to the Philharmonic for its jubilee.

"This Orchestra is a Rocket!"

In the foyer of the Haus der Musik stands a sculpture over fifteen feet tall made of traveling cases for instruments. It is entitled *Special Cases—Cosmic Rocket* and was created by the Austrian artist Nives Widauer. (The director of the Haus der Musik, Simon Posch, was delighted that the letters WPH imprinted on the cases read HdM when turned upside-down, the

One founder and four Chairs: Andreas Großbauer, Walter Barylli,
Clemens Hellsberg and Werner Resel with the portrait of Otto Nicolai

A ceremonial moment in the Haus der Musik: in the first row: Dominique Meyer, Margit and Heinz Fischer, Andreas Großbauer, Christa Ludwig and Walter Barylli

Anyone who shows no sign of fatigue must be getting enough sleep—and not on stage, either, for the following anecdote is in no way based on a true event. One Philharmoniker says to the other: “Know what I dreamed the other night? I am sitting on stage at the Musikverein and playing Beethoven!”—“What’s so special about that?”— “When I wake up…I am sitting on stage at the Musikverein and playing Beethoven!” Pace the 27th Psalm, but: no way does “the Lord give his beloved sleep.” “I don’t think they work as much on a mid-ocean oil platform,” says violist Thilo Fechner (Merz).

Dominique Meyer’s favorite anecdote reflects an unbendable will to work. He met Rainer Küchl once after a subscription concert in the Musikverein, where Zubin Mehta had just conducted Bruckner’s Ninth. Küchl, shaking his head, said: “This morning I played in the Hofmusikkapelle, and just now this fabulous concert, but still, I am sad. Because tonight at the State Opera is the last performance of *Lady Macbeth of Mtsensk*—and I didn’t get assigned to it!”

Regular Sunday duty for church music in the Hofburg is one more element in the jam-packed calendar of our orchestra. The Hofmusikkapelle (the former Court Orchestra) is one of the oldest musical institutions in the world; its founding dates back to the fifteenth century. For the musicians, recruited from the ranks of the Court or State Opera Orchestra, this work was once a plum job: an extra salary with a pension, a uniform with a bicorn hat, personal coach transportation on Sunday morning with a liveried servant carrying your instrument for you. Uniform and coach are gone, but the duty remains.

Rainer Küchl retired from his life position in summer of 2016—after a record service of 46 years as Philharmonic concertmaster (exceeded only by Rosé with 57 years as concertmaster, but at the State Opera only). To the next generation of orchestra players, Küchl passes along this challenge to stay unconditionally motivated: “I tell my younger colleagues over and over: Don’t gripe about too much work! The opportunity to play so much good music, material rewards aside, is priceless!” (Merz)

Orchestra stage manager Martin Stangl in action

New Chairman Daniel Froschauer with Elisabeth Khevenhüller-Metsch of the Artistic Business Office and stage manager Thomas Smula

And the Future?

Karl Böhm's words at the 125th anniversary of the Vienna Philharmonic in 1967 remain valid today: "The double function of the orchestra in the opera and in the concert hall is certainly a difficult and exhausting job, and for that reason demands complete commitment, because it requires mastery of the whole repertory. Nonetheless, it is an intelligent, good, even outstanding arrangement, and even more than that: it is the foundation without which the realization of the Philharmonic idea is not possible. It is only from the secure financial platform of opera engagements that we can jump off into free Philharmonic music-making as we understand it." But will structures and institutions that were without doubt secure half a century ago continue into the future indefinitely? And can the bow of high achievement be stretched too far?

Franz Bartolomey was never inclined to laziness: not for nothing does he say this Goethe aphorism is his favorite quotation: "Life is a struggle: fortunate are they who do not tire." Still, there is a little Philharmonic self-criticism in Bartolomey's memoirs: he mentions "ever more pressured tour planning" and "too little time to recover and relax," which are not good for the quality. "So it is becoming a growing challenge for those in charge to find the right balance between marketing and that highest artistic standard."

Merlin opens up another possibility, which of course has a prerequisite: increased funding. The "enormous workload" makes a further increase in the number of positions worth considering. For "with 148 members, the orchestra of the Vienna State Opera has 26 fewer planned positions than the Paris Opera with 174 orchestra members, who deal with 191 performances during the season while in Vienna, the State Opera and the Philharmonic together offer 406 evenings."

With respect to the relationship of the State Opera to its orchestra, one could speak of mutual "dependency," of strains and limitations, but also of cross-fertilization and mutual inspiration—and not just because a jubilee requires us to be optimistic.

The last speech on March 28, 2017, was given by Ex-Chair Clemens Hellsberg. He confessed that not every day of the job had been "fun," but that he had had important companions like Business Manager Dieter

Flury at his side. “But the most important companion,” said Hellsberg, “was the music. I have always felt nurtured and protected by the music of the masters. They took paths that we would not have found—but we may follow them confidently. Let us continue on this path, trusting that we are being well led.”

And so, 175 years after its founding, we hope, for them and for us, that this orchestra will confidently continue on the path of music for all its future. In the documentary feature by Merz, Daniel Barenboim formulated this hope: “As long as there is any kind of civilized society, the Vienna Philharmonic will be there.”

The Vienna Philharmonic Orchestra

Members in the Jubilee Season 2016/2017

* Member of the work group *(Arbeitsgemeinschaft)* of the Vienna Philharmonic

CONCERTMASTER
Rainer Honeck
Volkhard Steude
Albena Danailova

FIRST VIOLIN
Hubert Kroisamer
Josef Hell
Jun Keller
Daniel Froschauer
Maxim Brilinsky
Erich Schagerl
Milan Šetena
Martin Kubik
Martin Zalodek
Kirill Kobantschenko
Wilfried Hedenborg
Johannes Tomböck
Isabelle Ballot
Andreas Großbauer
Pavel Kuzmichev
Olesya Kurylyak
Thomas Küblböck
Alina Pinchas
Alexandr Sorokow*
Petra Kovačič*
Ekaterina Frolova*

SECOND VIOLIN
Raimund Lissy
Tibor Kovác
Christoph Koncz
Gerald Schubert
Helmut Zehetner
Patricia Hood-Koll
George Fritthum
Alexander Steinberger
René Staar
Harald Krumpöck
Michal Kostka
Benedict Lea
Marian Lesko
Johannes Kostner
Martin Klimek
Jewgenij Andrusenko
Shkëlzen Doli
Holger Groh
Adela Frasineanu*
Benjamin Morrison*

VIOLA
Heinrich Koll
Tobias Lea
Christian Frohn
Wolf-Dieter Rath
Robert Bauerstatter
Gerhard Marschner

Mario Karwan
Martin Lemberg
Elmar Landerer
Innokenti Grabko
Michael Strasser
Ursula Ruppe
Thilo Fechner
Thomas Hajek
Daniela Ivanova
Sebastian Führlinger
Tilman Kühn*

VIOLONCELLO
Tamás Varga
Robert Nagy
Peter Somodari
Raphael Flieder
Csaba Bornemisza
Sebastian Bru
Gerhard Iberer
Wolfgang Härtel
Eckart Schwarz-Schulz
Stefan Gartmayer
Ursula Wex
Edison Pashko
Bernhard Hedenborg
David Pennetzdorfer*

DOUBLE BASS
Herbert Mayr
Christoph Wimmer
Ödön Rácz
Jerzy (Jurek) Dybal
Itzok Hrastnik
Filip Waldmann
Alexander Matschinegg
Michael Bladerer
Bartosz Sikorski
Jan Georg Leser
Jędrzej Górski
Elias Mai

HARP
Charlotte Balzereit
Anneleen Lenaerts

FLUTE
Dieter Flury
Walter Auer
Karl-Heinz Schütz
Günter Federsel
Wolfgang Breinschmid
Karin Bonelli

OBOE
Martin Gabriel
Clemens Horak
Harald Hörth
Alexander Öhlberger
Wolfgang Plank
Herbert Maderthaner

CLARINET
Ernst Ottensamer († 22nd July 2017)
Matthias Schorn
Daniel Ottensamer
Norbert Täubl
Andreas Wieser
Gregor Hinterreiter*

BASSOON
Štěpán Turnovský
Harald Müller
Sophie Dartigalongue*
Michael Werba
Wolfgang Koblitz
Benedikt Dinkhauser

HORN
Ronald Janezic
Josef Reif
Manuel Huber
Sebastian Mayr
Wolfgang Lintner
Jan Janković
Wolfgang Vladar
Thomas Jöbstl
Wolfgang Tomböck
Lars Michael Stransky

TRUMPET
Martin Mühlfellner
Stefan Haimel
Jürgen Pöchhacker
Hans Peter Schuh
Reinhold Ambros
Gotthard Eder

TROMBONE
Dietmar Küblböck
Wolfgang Strasser
Johann Ströcker
Mark Gaal

TUBA
Paul Halwax
Christoph Gigler

PERCUSSION
Anton Mittermayr
Erwin Falk
Thomas Lechner
Klaus Zauner
Oliver Madas
Benjamin Schmidinger

RETIRED MEMBERS OF THE VIENNA PHILHARMONIC (AS OF 14TH AUGUST 2017)
Volker Altmann
Roland Baar
Franz Bartolomey
Walter Barylli
Georg Bedry
Roland Berger
Bernhard Biberauer
Walter Blovsky
Gottfried Boisits
Wolfgang Brand
Rudolf Degen
Reinhard Dürrer
Alfons Egger
Friedrich Faltl
Jörgen Fog
Gerhard Formanek
Herbert Frühauf
Wolfram Görner
Peter Götzel
Dietfried Gürtler
Wolfgang Gürtler
Heinz Hanke
Bruno Hartl
Richard Heintzinger
Clemens Hellsberg

Wolfgang Herzer
Johann Hindler
Werner Hink
Günter Högner
Roland Horvath
Josef Hummel
Willibald Janezic
Karl Jeitler
Rudolf Josel
Erich Kaufmann
Gerhard Kaufmann
Harald Kautzky
Burkhard Kräutler
Rainer Küchl
Edward Kudlak
Manfred Kuhn
Walter Lehmayer
Anna Lelkes
Gerhard Libensky
Erhard Litschauer
Günter Lorenz
Gabriel Madas
William Mcelheney
Horst Münster
Rudolf J. Nekvasil
Hans Novak
Hans Peter Ochsenhofer
Reinhard Öhlberger
Ortwin Ottmaier
Peter Pecha
Friedrich Pfeiffer
Josef Pomberger
Kurt Prihoda
Helmuth Puffler
Reinhard Repp
Werner Resel
Milan Sagat
Herbert Schmid
Rudolf Schmidinger
Peter Schmidl
Wolfgang Schuster
Eckhard Seifert
Günter Seifert
Reinhold Siegl
Walter Singer
Helmut Skalar
Franz Söllner
Anton Straka
Gerhard Turetschek
Martin Unger
Peter Wächter
Hans-Wolfgang Weihs
Helmut Weiss
Alfred Welt
Ewald Winkler
Dietmar Zeman

Literature

Bartolomey, Franz: „Was zählt, ist der Augenblick". Die Bartolomeys. 120 Jahre an der Wiener Staatsoper, Wien 2012
Blaukopf, Herta und Kurt: Die Wiener Philharmoniker. Wesen—Werden—Wirken eines großen Orchesters, Wien 1986
Burghauser, Hugo: Philharmonische Begegnungen. Erinnerungen eines Wiener Philharmonikers, Zürich 1979
Gallup, Stephen: A History of the Salzburg Festival, o. O. 1988
Halwax, Paul (Hg.): Ball der Wiener Philharmoniker, Wien 2016
Hellsberg, Clemens: Demokratie der Könige. Die Geschichte der Wiener Philharmoniker, Zürich/Wien/Mainz 1992
Kralik, Heinrich: Das große Orchester. Die Wiener Philharmoniker und ihre Dirigenten, Wien 1952
Lammerhuber, Lois (Hg.): Passion. Wiener Staatsopernorchester. Wiener Philharmoniker, Wien 2011
Mayrhofer, Bernadette/Trümpi, Fritz: Orchestrierte Vertreibung. Unerwünschte Wiener Philharmoniker. Verfolgung, Ermordung und Exil, Wien 2014
Merlin, Christian: Die Wiener Philharmoniker. I: Das Orchester und seine Geschichte von 1842 bis heute. II: Die Musiker und Musikerinnen von 1842 bis heute, Wien 2017
Rathkolb, Oliver: „Führertreu und gottbegnadet". Künstlereliten im Dritten Reich, Wien 1991
Sachs, Harvey (Hg.): Arturo Toscanini dal 1915 al 1946. L'arte all'ombra della politica, Torino 1987
Strasser, Otto: Sechse is. Wie ein Orchester musiziert und funktioniert, Wien 1981
Strasser, Otto: Und dafür wird man noch bezahlt. Mein Leben mit den Wiener Philharmonikern, Wien 1974
Weigel, Hans: Das Buch der Wiener Philharmoniker, Salzburg 1967
Weingartner, Felix: Lebenserinnerungen, Wien 1923
Die Wiener Philharmoniker: Mehr als Musik, directed by Co Merz, C2M Production, 2016 (TV documentary feature)
Witeschnik, Alexander: Musizieren geht übers Probieren, Wien 1967
Wrochem, Oliver von (Hg.): Nationalsozialistische Täterschaften. Nachwirkungen in Gesellschaft und Familie, Berlin 2016

Photo credits

Vienna Philharmonic Orchestra/Benedikt Dinkhauser (14, 116, 126, 128/129, 131 bottom, 153 bottom, 159 bottom, 164, 181, 203 above, 209), Dr. Otto Böhler/Archives of the Vienna Philharmonic Orchestra (16, 55 unten), Historical Archive of the Vienna Philharmonic Orchestra (24, 27, 30, 35, 38/39, 50/51, 53 bottom, 56, 60, 67, 70/71, 75 bottom, 78, 83 above, 83 bottom right, 86, 89, 91, 96, 97, 101, 106, 107, 111, 134, 135, 138, 141, 170, 171, 176 above 1st left, 176 bottom left, 177 above 1st right), Gerhard Trumler/IMAGNO/picturedesk.com (31, 148), Archive of Amalthea Publishing Company (37, 53 above, 55 above), Harry Weber/ÖNB-Bildarchiv/picturedesk.com (44), Historical Archive of the Vienna Philharmonic Orchestra/Photo L. Grillich (49), Max Oppenheimer/IMAGNO/picturedesk.com (64/65), Arnold Schönberg Center, Vienna (75 above), Austrian Archives/IMAGNO/picturedesk.com (83 bottom left, 99), Elfriede Hanak, Vienna (131 above), Vienna Philharmonic Orchestra/Martin Kubik (132, 153 above), Vienna Philharmonic Orchestra/Jun Keller (143, 153 centre), Suntory Hall (156/157, 159 above), Vienna Philharmonic Orchestra/Terry Linke (158 above, 163, 176 above 2nd left, 176 bottom centre, 177 above 2nd right, 177 bottom right, 190 bottom, 198, 199), Vienna Philharmonic Orchestra/Richard Schuster (158 bottom, 192/193), Barbara Pflaum/IMAGNO/picturedesk.com (190 above), Franz Hubmann/IMAGNO/picturedesk.com (195), Vienna Philharmonic Orchestra/Wilfried Hedenborg (203 bottom)

The following illustrations have been borrowed from "Was zählt, ist der Augenblick. Die Bartolomeys. 120 Jahre an der Wiener Staatsoper" by Franz Bartolomey (Amalthea, Vienna 2012): private archive Franz Bartolomey/Photo L. Grillich (142 left), private archive Franz Bartolomey (142 centre, 166), Richard Schuster (142 right)
Photo taken in the concert hall Musiikkitalo/Helsinki: Vienna Philharmonic Orchestra/Benedikt Dinkhauser (185)

page 23: map © arbeitsgemeinschaft kartographie/mblue.at Graphic and Webdesign e. U., photo Musikverein © Gesellschaft der Musikfreunde in Wien/Wolf-Dieter Grabner, photo State Opera © Vienna State Opera/Michael Pöhn, photo Sacher © Hotel Sacher Vienna, photo Haus der Musik © Haus der Musik/Inge Prader
front endpaper: Terry Linke
back endpaper: Lois Lammerhuber

Index of persons

GESELLSCHA